COLLEGE SURVIVAL

Greg Gottesman, Daniel Baer, and Friends

THOMSON
ARCO

Australia • Canada • Mexico • Singapore • Spain • United Kingdom • United States

Dedication

To my grandma, who taught me so much.—G.G.

For my aunt, Dr. Teddi Baer (yes that was her real name),
whose life was cut short but fully lived.—D.B.

Table of Contents

ABOUT THE AUTHORS

Greg Gottesman graduated from Stanford University with a degree in political science and from Harvard Law School and Harvard Business School. He now lives in Seattle with his wife, Shannon, and son, Zack. Greg and Shannon are the authors of *Law School Survival*, a survival guide for law school students by law school students. Greg is also the editor of *High School Survival*, a survival guide for high school students. In his free time, Greg enjoys going to movies and playing tennis and golf.

Daniel Baer is a recent graduate of Harvard University, where he majored in social and political theory as well as Afro-American Studies. He wrote for the *Harvard Political Review* and is active in an after-school program for elementary school children in the Boston area. He loves to write, ski, and hang out with his family.

THE ADVENTURES OF JOE D. ZASTER

ACKNOWLEDGMENTS

College Survival now enters its sixth edition, which hopefully will be as successful as the last five. Truthfully, I was happy just to see it make it to edition number one. It has survived with—to borrow a phrase from the Beatles —(more than) a little help from my friends.

For this sixth edition, I want to thank Roy Opochinski, a developmental editor at Peterson's, who spent time updating, editing, and trying to improve the book. Jennifer Gordon, an editor at Peterson's, also was a great help in making sure that the sixth edition improved upon the fifth.

Daniel Baer, a very recent graduate of Harvard, joined the fifth edition as co-author. His chapter on the Internet and his revisions were timely and excellent. I feel fortunate to have such a talented co-author and friend.

Most of *College Survival* has stayed exactly the same as when we wrote it in my freshman and sophomore years at Stanford University. Once again, let me thank the people who made the first edition possible.

Reliable sources tell me that my mom actually came up with the idea for *College Survival*. Both my parents helped edit the book, especially my mom. My dad was particularly helpful in editing the computer chapter and in adding some corny jokes.

My journalist grandma, Mary K. Brown, to whom the book is dedicated, gave me some solid advice during every phase of the book. I'm embarrassed to say how many of my high school English papers she corrected.

My friend, Steve Ojemann, who is now a brain surgeon (no joke!), drew all the wonderful cartoons. Thank you for your great wit, Steve.

Chip Shields, a high school counselor and author of *The College Guide to Parents*, deserves much of the credit for helping me get this book published. I also want to thank some friends at ARCO, Linda Bernbach and Christina Buffamonte, for all their help, patience, and wisdom. Lisa Bianchi was especially helpful in organizing the first edition. Don Essig, an editor at ARCO, did great work on the fifth edition.

The heart and soul of this book, however, belongs to the contributors. I especially would like to thank the following students for their extensive work in these areas: Rico Alexander on packing, Rick Arney and Stanley Ryter on banking, Christina Buffamonte on commuting, Bryan Cohen on partying, Dr. Lauren Warchal Cohen on community colleges, Matt Crile on Greek versus dorm life,

Andy Gottesman on choosing classes and orientation, Leslie Friend on health, nutrition, and Greek versus dorm life, Tara McCann on getting involved, Whitney Morris on what to bring for your dorm room, Thom McDade on time management, Tami Ostroff on clothing, John Pilafidis and Jamie Reynolds on computers, John Schreuder on working at school, David Stern on cars, Martina Stewart on the minority experience, Keith Vernon on athletics and exercise, Noeleen Walder on campus safety, and Jessica Hall on roommates.

Thanks to all the college students whose true stories give the book its unique spirit. For answering important questions and working on parts of chapters, I want to thank Dr. Jeff Tauben, Dr. Nancy Schuette, Ethan Diamond, Maureen Strasser, and Paddy Carson. Alita Kiaer, my favorite English teacher, always deserves special mention. And to the many people at the health clinics, department stores, libraries, Laundromats, airlines, packing centers, and service stations, thank you too.

Saving the best for last, I want to thank my wife, Shannon, and son, Zack, who didn't mind me spending much of my vacation time editing this new edition. I always have a lot of fun trying to make the book just a little bit better.

—Greg Gottesman

Thanks to Greg for all his help and guidance on this project, and to Linda Bernbach for helping facilitate this "group effort."

Thanks to my roommates Conan and Dave, without whom I would not survive college. Thanks to Sarah for her unfailing friendship, support, and love. And to all my friends at school whose advice and support I trust and rely on.

Most of all, thanks to my family.

—Daniel Baer

PREFACE

"In my end is my beginning."

—T. S. Eliot

For many, getting that fat envelope in the mail is a relief. And why not? A college acceptance letter invariably symbolizes the end of four long years of high school. No more fights with dad over keys to the car. No more arguments with mom about "independence." Indeed, no more worrying about who you are going to spend Homecoming with or who you are going to sit with in the school cafeteria.

But don't let anyone fool you. College is by no means an end to your jaded past; in fact, it is more of a beginning. It is the beginning of learning to be responsible, independent, and street smart. Balancing a checkbook, washing dirty clothes, deciding what to bring to school, making your own airline reservations, choosing between a fraternity and a dormitory, communicating with a roommate about his or her "hygiene habits," interior decorating . . . these are all mountains that each college student will at one time or another attempt to conquer.

This book, written by college kids from all over the country, will not give you all the answers to university life; what it will give you are facts, accurate information, and alternatives. It will tell you how to avoid the woes of a college freshman who was forced to wear dull pink the entire fall quarter. It will give you tips on college dating and surfing the Internet. It will familiarize you with the wrong and right things to pack up for East, West, and Midwest travel. It will teach you about hundreds of other things every college freshman should know before taking the big plunge.

The following pages offer an education, not just in a classroom sense, but in a life sense as well. As Mark Twain once said, "Don't let school get in the way of your education."

Twain never was a student.

Good luck.

CHAPTER 1

Clothing: What to Bring

❝ *I love clothes, cosmetics, socks, shoes . . . heck, I love just about everything you can put in a suitcase. No wonder I had problems packing for college.*

After making trips to the back-to-school sale at Nordstrom and the local discount drugstore, I raced home—the moment of truth had arrived. First I made a few neat piles on the floor, but soon I abandoned that method and started throwing everything into the empty bags. Next thing you know, my bags were ready to burst, not even enough space for a few pairs of underwear.

'Wait a second!' I thought to myself. 'What in the world did I pack? Did I forget socks?'

Luckily, you always can empty your bags and start again. But it's probably smarter to pack in an orderly fashion the first time."

—Tami Ostroff, Pomona College

 Psst . . . For your convenience, a tear-out checklist with all your packing essentials appears on pages **235–243**. Please refer to it as you go through Chapters 1 and 2.

The Don'ts Of Packing College Clothing

1. DON'T OVERPACK.

Take what you know you will wear. The stuff you think you "might" wear, you won't! Plus, if you're used to having tons of storage space at home, think again! You won't have room to be a packrat. It's best to take only what you know you will wear. You can always bring additional items to school later. Or, if you have five pairs of jeans, leave a couple at home for school breaks.

A few ways to judge if you've overpacked: Can you zip your suitcase? Can you carry the suitcases to the car? Do the front wheels of the car lift off the ground when the trunk is loaded? Is the airline willing to ship your bags with no additional freight charges? Most airlines allow two checked bags that weigh no more than 70 pounds each. If you have a question about your airline's policy, call its toll-free number, which you can find in your phone book or by calling information at 800-555-1212.

2. DON'T PACK FOR THE BAHAMAS. REMEMBER THE CLIMATE.

Are you going to Tempe, Arizona or Ithaca, New York? Did you take enough Bermuda shorts or heavy sweaters? Did you take too many?

Climate should play a major role in wardrobe decisions.

3. DON'T PACK MOM'S FAVORITES.

❝ *Being a last-minute person, I was in a crunch when it came time to pack for college. My mom ended up doing the majority of packing for me. What a mistake!*

Instead of packing what I wanted, I ended up with my mom's favorites. I had these wool sweaters, which were about as comfortable as the neck brace from my orthodontist. I had too many nice T-shirts and nothing to play basketball in. When I drove home a few weekends later, I had to do the whole packing thing over again."

—Dan Gottesman, University of Washington

Pack what you will be comfortable wearing. You won't wear mom's favorites once at school.

4. DON'T PACK A LOT OF CLOTHES THAT NEED DRY CLEANING OR IRONING.

Ironing is a pain and hand-washing is totally out of the question.

Consider easy-care, "wrinkle-free" fabrics. Although 100 percent cotton and 100 percent wool are chic, they require extra care.

5. DON'T BE SOMEONE ELSE.

If you have your own style of dress, don't be afraid to show it. At college, individuality is admired just as much as conformity. In fact, nonconformist attire is often trendy on college campuses.

6. DON'T FORGET TO CHECK THE BATHROOM AND BEDROOM DRAWERS.

Before leaving, take a walk around your bedroom and bathroom. If you see any drawers still unopened, you probably have forgotten something. Check again.

Underwear, Socks, Pajamas, etc.

Underwear is always the first thing you run out of. Bring lots. Socks, too! You don't want to be doing a wash every five days.

A big terry-cloth bathrobe, especially for women, may be a lifesaver on coed floors. The walk from the shower to your room may be quite a hike.

Depending on your sleepwear style, you may want to bring a few pairs of cotton/flannel pajama pants to school. Not only will they be comfy for sleeping, but they make great loungewear for hanging out around the dorm or late-night study sessions.

Casual Wear

Of course, what you bring should depend foremost on your personal style and on the climate in which you will be living.

But blue jeans, khakis, T-shirts, and sweatshirts receive an extra "thumbs up" because of their versatility. In addition, it's hard to beat sweats and a baseball cap when you are late for a 9 A.M. class. If your high school was one where students were extremely attentive to their appearance, don't expect college to be the same. Some people still dress nicely, but if you show up in class without makeup or with a five o'clock shadow, you won't be alone. Minimizing the amount of time between rolling out of bed and arriving at class is a finely honed skill for many college students!

Remember light (such as white) clothes will keep you cooler in hot climates because they reflect the sun's heat.

Bathroom Buddies: Towels and Cosmetics

66 *It seemed at least half my graduation gifts were not checks or pens but towels. I began wondering whether my friends thought I was dirty or needed to shower more often. In any case, I took nearly all the towels to school with me. They turned out to be a great graduation gift."*

—Whitney Morris, Pomona College

You will want at least three or four big bath towels and maybe another for sunbathing and one or two washcloths.

You might want to invest $3.99 in a small crate or tackle-box-type container that you can put your toiletries/cosmetics in for easy transport back and forth from the bathroom.

Shoes

Shoes hog suitcase space. Take only what you will wear. Also, remember the climate in which you will be residing: Sandals are more practical in California than in North Dakota. And if you are live in Miami and are going to school in Minnesota, you will find better deals and selection on climate-specific footwear (for example, snow boots) once you get to school.

Jewelry

Be especially careful with your valuable jewelry. Don't bring a diamond Rolex unless you are feeling charitable. Remember that your roommate might not be as careful about locking the doors as you are.

Formal Wear

You are going to need some nice-looking duds for job interviews, religious services, or formals, but not necessarily a tuxedo or an evening gown.

If you don't have a tuxedo and one is required, you can always rent one. You can also ask upperclassmen how many times you will need a tuxedo. Depending on what they say, you might find it more cost-efficient to buy one. For the most part, though, "formal" collegiate gatherings require a sports jacket—nothing more! A navy blue blazer and khakis or gray slacks are usually a sure bet on any campus.

> 66 *I only brought one of my fancy dresses to college. Girls who bring more are just asking for trouble. First of all, you are always going to have problems with storage, especially in sororities. Chances are, your dress will be mushed in between all your other stuff. Besides, if you are ever in a crunch, you can always borrow a dress from a friend. They usually don't mind as long as you return the favor."*
>
> —Stephanie Sleight, Oregon State University

Women will probably want to bring at least one formal dress to college. If you don't like to wear dresses more than a few times, trading with friends is more than acceptable.

Outerwear for Colder Climates

"Don't be stuck in a Chicago winter without a good pair of gloves," warns Leslie Friend, a senior at the University of Chicago.

Gloves are not the only thing you will need, particularly if you like to ski or plan on attending school in a colder climate. Consult the tear-out checklist in the back of this book. And remember that it may be better to shop for these items once you get to school.

Medical Supplies

A well-stocked first aid kit can save you a trip to the infirmary. Since storage space may be limited, determine which items are most necessary.

You can pick up an Emergency Supply Kit from the American Red Cross for roughly $20.

Be sure to make any necessary arrangements for any prescription medications that you require. Consult your physician before you go.

Sports Gear

Depending on your sport, you may need certain gear (squash racket, snorkel gear, golf clubs, and so on). Plan on bringing a few of the basics. For example, you might want a mitt for the inevitable dorm softball game or a tennis racket in case there's a court down the street. Remember that people will probably ask to borrow whatever you bring, so you might not want to bring any equipment that you don't feel comfortable lending.

CHAPTER 2

Your Room: What to Bring

❝ *When I packed for college last fall, I filled an entire U-Haul trailer with loads of junk that for one reason or another I was convinced I would need. I was sending tons of clothing, extra ski equipment, a teapot, a spare flashlight . . . to name a few.*

Needless to say, end-of-the-year packing was sheer misery. I was still at it when my parents arrived to escort me home. I thought I would never leave Pomona. The moral of the story: Take less rather than more. It's amazing all the things you really don't need."

—Whitney Morris, Pomona College

Take Less Rather Than More!

This chapter should help transform your dormitory room into your castle. Keep these things in mind:

1. You are going to be living there for one year, not a lifetime. College rooms are smaller than you think.

2. Check with your future roommate. Two radios are too many. Two televisions are too many. So are two phones. Avoid duplication.

3. Unless you are going to school in the boonies, a store with everything you could ever need is bound to be around the corner. Don't worry!

4. You are bound to have a list of things that you want to buy for your dorm room. Don't forget about used items—garage sales and thrift stores can be a college student's treasure chest.

Bed Basics

You should consider a washable spread, as your bed will become a couch, a study lounge, and a footrest to all who enter. If you are going to school in a colder climate, you might want a down or wool comforter. You can buy removable and washable comforter/duvet covers at any department store.

Check with your school to determine whether the beds are *regular length* or *extra-long*. Regular-sized flat sheets can be used on an extra-long mattress, but fitted sheets must be purchased in the extra-long size. You can get extra-long twin sheets from some catalogues as well as some national chains.

Check to see if your school has a linen or laundry service. Some schools even provide students with clean sheets and towels each week.

If you have room to store it, bring a sleeping bag. You may want to camp in the surrounding woodland or lend the bag to a visiting friend.

Your Academic Headquarters: School Supplies

Pens and pencils like to get up and walk away; a storage bin will keep them where they belong. Also, you might want to grab a few highlighters—college means much more reading.

You will need a backpack, preferably a large bag, to carry all your junk to class. Over-the-shoulder canvas attachés and satchels also make good book bags. If you're looking for one, check out your local army surplus store.

Books

You will be buying a whole slew of textbooks at school, but there are a few essential reference books you can bring from home.

- ❏ A respected dictionary (the most recent edition)
  Suggestion: *Webster's New World*
- ❏ A foreign-language dictionary, if you plan to study a language
  Suggestion: *Harper Collins Robert*
- ❏ A thesaurus or synonym-finder, preferably in easy-to-use dictionary form
  Suggestion: *Roget's International Thesaurus*
  (Note: Microsoft Word contains this feature and an online thesaurus can be found at www.thesaurus.com.)
- ❏ The Bible, not necessarily for religious purposes

❏ A book on the rules of English grammar
Suggestion: *The Elements of Style* by William Strunk, Jr. and E.B. White

❏ A book of quotations
Suggestion: *Bartlett's Book of Quotations*

❏ MLA Guide to Documentation
This is an invaluable tool for writing bibliographies and footnote citations.

Lighting

Mom was right. Reading in the dark does strain your eyes and may trigger headaches. So, if you plan to study, don't be lazy: Get out of bed and turn on the light.

Large floor lamps take up too much space. Get a good reading lamp for your bed and one for your desk.

Because they produce enough heat to ignite flammable items, halogen lamps are now forbidden at many schools.

Making Extra Space: Storage, Closets and Organization

❝ *Two beds can barely fit into some of the rooms at Stanford, let alone two people. So, instead of living like sardines, I decided to do something about it and built a loft.*

With the loft in place, my roommate and I had loads of space. We had room for the stereo, a futon, plants, more shelves . . . more everything. With just a few pieces of wood and a power saw, I turned our once humble shanty into a palace, of sorts."

—Alex Berzins, Stanford University

You will not have much space, so be creative when organizing and planning ahead.

A large trunk serves various functions; it can act as a large suitcase, a table, or a base for stacking other storage units.

Baskets perform an assortment of roles as well: shelves, drawers, cupboards, and shoe holders, to name a few. Crates work equally well.

Bookshelves are great space savers. Check your room first. The school may have already installed plenty of shelves. If not, head for the nearest lumber yard, furniture outlet, or Home Depot and buy or build what you need. Also, if you have a large CD collection, you might want to consider putting your CDs into storage albums. They will be easier to transport and take up less room on your bookshelf at school.

Plastic storage bins might be particularly useful. You can get them in sizes that fit under a bed—in college there's no room for wasted space.

If space is really a problem, you can always build a loft and get rid of one of the beds. Former students are usually in the business of selling their old lofts. For around $50, it may be a good investment, especially if you don't feel like (or can't) build your own.

Curing the Munchies

66 *During my freshman year, my roommate and I managed to lure half of the water polo team into our room with the scent of popcorn. After this encouraging beginning, we employed the popper frequently, but never again with such success."*

—Erin Charles, UC Berkeley

Check with your dormitory, fraternity, or sorority before purchasing any appliances. Many dorms have kitchens with refrigerators, ovens, and microwaves for student use. Also, coordinate with your roommate—no need for two toaster ovens. A refrigerator, hotpot, cups, and kitchen utensils are especially recommended—if the school does not provide them.

 Psst . . . In some schools, electrical appliances such as hot pots are contraband because they are considered fire hazards. You might want to check on your school's policy before buying one.

The Dilemma With Refrigerators: To Rent or Buy?

Nearly every college in the western hemisphere has commissioned a local organization to rent refrigerators on a semester or yearly basis. The company generally offers the square, 1.6 cubic foot size as well as the larger, rectangular 2.8 cubic foot size. Costs vary, but $50–$100 dollars per year is standard. Split between two or three people, the fee becomes more manageable.

Buying a new refrigerator at Sears or a local discount appliance store will run around $100–$150. Over the long haul, this is the more reasonable investment, but you must deal with summer storage and come up with the initial expense. You also must provide your own maintenance.

Renting the first year and then purchasing a used fridge from a graduating senior may be your best bet.

Five Quick Tips for Decorating Your Castle

" *The most memorable room I saw during my freshman year belonged to an unlikely pair of roommates, Brenda and Aileen. Although they had different tastes in almost every area, they managed to coordinate their styles and create a lively environment in a tiny space.*

They bought some tacky dime-store beads, which hung in strings in the doorway. In the place of honor on the fridge sat a lava lamp named Sybil. Posters of Billy Idol's leering grin were interspersed with posters of The Cure and Monet prints.

Even the ceiling had a special touch. A student who was an astronomy major had lived in the room several years earlier and had positioned glow-in-the-dark stars all over the ceiling. You could lie on the floor and look at actual constellations.

Many a social gathering took place in their humble abode, partly because of the women and partly because of the environment they had created."

—Whitney Morris, Pomona College

Don't Expect Paradise

Upon arrival, don't entertain delusions of your new room looking like Trump Palace. The Gobi desert would be more apropos.

But all is not lost. A few decorating tips, a few inspired ideas, a few nails, and who knows? *Better Homes and Gardens* beware!

1. POSTERS AND PICTURES ADD PIZAZZ TO ANY WALL.

Posters are easy to find, easy to put up, and even easier on the pocketbook.

Hometown favorites, from a county fair or your city's skyline, attach a local flavor to the room. University stores have huge assortments. Monet prints are especially popular.

Pictures of family and friends can do more than cure hometown blues. They can add life to a wall, a dresser, or a desk.

Magazine covers can also spruce up a wall, so rip the covers off that pile of *Sports Illustrated* issues that you have in the bathroom. They make for cheap wallpaper.

2. A BULLETIN BOARD IS NEVER TACK-Y.

Along with helping you organize, bulletin boards provide a perfect medium for placing photos you have taken during the year. A bulletin board also means you don't have to bombard your walls with numerous large nails.

 Psst . . . Many schools have rules that disallow the use of nails or pins in walls. Find out about your school's policy before you pick up a hammer. Move cautiously as fines are often steep. If there is a prohibition on nails, then go to your local hardware store and pick up some non-permanent adhesive.

3. THROW-RUGS BEAT ANY DORMITORY FLOOR.

Although expensive, a rug can change the atmosphere of a room. Besides giving a cozy look, a rug provides actual warmth; it keeps the room and your toes comfortable. Check with graduating seniors and local carpet stores for the best deals.

4. DRESS UP YOUR WINDOWS.

Most dormitory windows come with some sort of covering. If not, you can make your own or buy inexpensive curtains or shades from variety stores. Budding artists have a field day with window treatments, all the way from laminated shades to bamboo rollers. A strand of white Christmas lights in the window will create a festive atmosphere.

5. DECORATE THE DOOR.

The quintessential door reflects the personality of those behind it. Crossed-out pictures of ex-boyfriends, rejection letters from rival universities, applications to greasy fast-food chains, articles about the World Wrestling Federation, parking tickets . . . put it all up!

> ❝ *This guy down the hall decorated his door with every article he could find relating to the reincarnation of Elvis Presley. I couldn't believe how much he found . . . definitely one of the funniest things I have ever seen."*
>
> —Greg Gottesman, Stanford University

You will need some writing apparatus near your door that allows others to leave messages. A note pad with a pencil on a string works well.

For a few more pennies (around $10 worth), you can splurge on an erasable message board.

 Psst . . . Remember who's living in the room and who's supposed to enjoy it. Beauty is in the eye of the beholder. But beware . . . decorations such as bare-all centerfolds may offend more people than they impress.

CHAPTER 3

Packing and Sending

66 *It was the day before my flight, so I was forced into a packing frenzy. I placed my stereo in a box of clothes and taped the box shut. I then preceded to—get this!—throw the box around the room. I figured if the box could withstand my punishment it certainly could weather whatever the airlines were about to dish out. What in the world was I thinking?*

When I opened the box, my stereo didn't work. How could it when it was in 100 pieces?"

—Rico Alexander, Stanford University

Boxes, Boxes, Boxes . . . Start in the Attic

For those who have never been in their attic, now is a good time. Skip over dad's old prom pictures and the broken transistor radios. You're looking for something else: cardboard boxes. Big boxes. Small boxes. Any and all boxes.

If the attic leaves you empty-handed, try the back alley of a warehouse or ask in a grocery or liquor store.

If you want to bypass the search altogether, purchase boxes from a packaging or moving company. This can get pricey, but it may be convenient to have boxes that are all the same size, and you can use them over and over again. Bicycle boxes can be picked up at bike shops or department stores for a minimal charge. If you decide to have your bike shipped, make sure that you know how to put it back together when you get to school.

The Scoop on Delivery Service: Rules for Potential Packers

The procedure for using a delivery service (such as UPS, Federal Express, DHL, and Emery) is pretty standard: Call the service, give them the address where you want the packages delivered, state the date you want it there, and estimate the weight of the packages involved. Then, pack your boxes and drop them at the local carrier. If cumbersome, the deliverer can pick up the goods at your house.

UPS provides a more complete set of guidelines, but these hints should take care of any "physical" packing problems.

1. Use cardboard boxes or a footlocker.
2. Protect items inside with crumpled grocery bags or special packing material (such as bubble wrap).
3. Place fragile items toward the middle of the box. The sides are more dangerous.
4. Close your boxes with tape two inches or greater in width. UPS recommends pressure-sensitive plastic or water-activated paper tape, but disapproves of string or rope.
5. Make sure to label the contents of your boxes. This way you can unpack in a systematic fashion. But avoid labels like "expensive electronics." These are always the first to get "lost in transit."

 Psst . . . If you are sending your worldly goods via a delivery service, set aside sufficient cosmetics, a few wardrobe changes, and a set of sheets and towels. You will want to keep these items with you because belongings don't always arrive as planned.

Packing Tips for Drivers

Driving to school is difficult enough without having to worry about the packing element. Follow these rules:

1. MAKE SURE THERE'S ENOUGH ROOM.

Don't be decapitated by the ski pole that couldn't fit in the back seat. Make sure your car has the space.

Laws forbid the obstruction of a driver's view with excess baggage. Keep the stuff in the back seat as low as possible.

When renting a car, ask for the largest size available. The difference in rates is minimal. Count family members as extra baggage. A grandma and two sisters equal about four large boxes.

2. IF SIZE IS A PROBLEM, RENT A U-HAUL TRAILER.

U-Haul trailers can turn small cars with no trunk space into all-purpose trucks, capable of lugging all your belongings to school.

Rates vary depending upon distance, time, and size of trailer. Mark, a manager of a U-Haul center, suggests a 4 × 8 trailer because it is more aerodynamic than the other sizes and therefore more fuel-efficient.

For a nominal fee, U-Haul will rent you trailer hitches, furniture pads, boxes, and protective locks.

3. KEEP A SEPARATE "TRAVEL BAG".

You will not want to go searching through boxes every night at a motel, so pack what you will need on the trip in a separate bag, and make sure that the bag is easily accessible.

Tips on Packing for Planes and Buses

66 *When I go back and forth between college and home, the only luggage I take is two big army duffel bags. They are so huge that even I can easily fit inside them, and they seem to hold endless amounts of stuff. Sure it's a pain lugging them around the airport, but it's only twice a year, and having the big bags means that I never have to ship anything to school—I can bring it all with me. It ends up saving me a lot of money and more than a few headaches."*

—Daniel Baer, Harvard University

If you are traveling by plane or train, remember to:

1. GO FOR CAPACITY, NOT FASHION.

When selecting baggage, you want the bags that can hold the most stuff, not Mom's set of matching luggage. If you don't already have a large duffel bag, you can pick one up at an army surplus store for about $25. If you are going to use more standard luggage, bags with wheels are nice, especially if you have to lug your stuff around campus trying to find your dorm.

2. FIND OUT THE RATES FOR EXTRA BAGGAGE.

Most airlines allow you to check two bags and carry one on board. The charge for each additional bag (or bicycle) is roughly $75.

Greyhound bus service allows two bags on-board and charges $15 for each additional bag. Bus companies may impose a five-bag maximum.

3. WATCH FOR WEIGHT LIMITS.

Greyhound has a 50-pound weight limit, while most airlines have 70-pound limits. If your boxes exceed the limit, look into delivery services. Remember that this limit is per bag—you can take two 70-pound bags, but not one 20-pounder and one 80-pounder.

4. CALL THE AIRLINE OR BUS COMPANY WITH SPECIAL CIRCUMSTANCES.

Some airlines and bus companies have special requirements with regard to packing certain items. For example, many airlines require you to use their special bicycle boxes, while others ask that you obtain your own. In these cases, calling the airline or bus company is your best bet.

What Are You Going to Do With All Your Stuff When the Year Ends?

66 *The first day when we moved in, my roommate's entire clan spent nearly an hour putting together this elaborate bathroom rack system for everybody's toiletries. For the record, it actually was incredibly useful for all of us. At the end of the year, Mark, not realizing that you can store stuff over the summer, had to figure out how to pack it up. There are two important things to realize about this monstrosity: (1) It has very long poles and bulky shelves, and (2) it is painfully heavy.*

After finally disassembling it, Mark had to cut apart six boxes and then literally create his own box by duct-taping the scraps together around the mess of poles and shelves. When he was done (an approximately two-hour procedure, meanwhile the rest of his belongings remained unpacked and his plane left in 3 hours), he had created a frightening cardboard-and-duct-tape behemoth that weighed over 60 pounds and rattled tremendously whenever moved. The Fed Ex guy looked at it, nudged it (resulting in more frightening crashes within what could no longer in any sense be called a 'box'), said that he couldn't accept it, and promptly left.

Now, you'll recall that time was running short for poor old Mark, so he called his dad to ask what he should do. Turns out, if you pay enough money, a Fed Ex man must accept any package. So the same guy returned with his tail between his legs and carted out the rapidly deteriorating concoction. Morals of the story: check to see the storage policies of your school; be reasonable and frugal about what you ship back and forth; duct tape and money can solve most any tough situation."

—David Sivak, Harvard University

When the year is over you will have to move out of your room before heading home. This poses a major challenge, especially if you have acquired various pieces of furniture, new clothing, and so on throughout the year.

Basically, you have two options: Store or ship.

1. **Storage.** Most schools will provide either free or low-cost storage to students who come from out of state. You should check into your school's policy, because there might be a limit on what you can store.

   If your school doesn't provide storage, you can go to a public-storage facility and ask about rates for summer storage. You might want to think about teaming up with a couple friends in this case. The cost of storage will be less when divided up, and you probably won't need a ton of space anyway. Plus, if there's a group of you, then you can all help each other load and unload.

2. **Ship.** Shipping your stuff back and forth between school and home can get expensive, but for some people, who simply cannot live without their 200-CD collection and their entire wardrobe, shipping is a necessary luxury. If you decide to ship your stuff home, check out rates of different companies before the last day. Also, do you need your stuff the next day or next week? There might be a big difference in cost if you are willing to wait a few extra days for delivery.

CHAPTER 4

Planes: Flying The Collegiate Skies

66 *I felt kind of guilty making my parents pay for my round-trip ticket home over winter break. 'I am a college man now,' I thought. It was one of those ego trips.*

Anyway, when the flight attendant announced that the plane might be overbooked, I dashed over to the counter to let her know that I was willing to give up my seat—for a free round-trip ticket, of course.

To make a short story shorter, I was booted off the flight and received a free round-trip ticket. The kicker was, the airline put me on another flight only 20 minutes later. My parents didn't even know I had been bumped. Even better, I had a great holiday present for my mom when she arrived at the airport—a free round-trip ticket."

Everett Hsu, Johns Hopkins University

Tips for Cheap, Smart Plane Travel

Before acing your first college final, before marching for liberal causes, before joining a sorority, before doing anything for that matter, you have to get there.

For those not within driving distance, the "getting there" facet of college life poses maj(air) problems. Maybe you have not flown much or maybe never at all. Maybe you do not know how to find the cheapest flights. Fear not! These next few hints should make "getting there" (through the air) as simple as one, two, three, four, five, six, seven, eight, and nine.

In addition to the following points, check out Chapter 13's discussion of the Internet for advice on using the Web to get travel deals!

Eight Tips on Plane Travel

1. GET A TRAVEL AGENT OR USE YOUR PARENTS' AGENT.

❝ *For spring break, my roommates and I wanted to go on a cruise. Instead of doing all the work ourselves, we called a travel agent near campus. Not only were his services free, he made all the reservations and saved us loads of time. He also found us the best rates—something I'm not sure I could have done.*

Even though my mom makes most of my plane reservations with our travel agent at home, I now know how easy it is to use one myself. It sure beats making all the arrangements yourself."

—Joellen Tapper, Occidental College

Travel agents can save you hundreds of dollars and hours of time. Better yet, many of them do not charge a penny, making all their commission from the airlines. Ask the travel agent if he or she charges a fee for service.

Since the deregulation of the airline industry, all carriers have been forced to compete for business. Standard fares do not exist today as they once did. In fact, Paul, a travel agent, explained that United Airlines offers seventeen— count'em, seventeen (17!)—different airfares between Seattle and New York alone, depending upon when you purchase the ticket, if the fare is non-refundable, what time you travel, what day of the week, if you are staying over a Saturday night, and which class you choose to fly.

Unless you do hours of research or employ a travel agent, finding the best fare from destination to destination is nearly impossible.

If you still don't believe it, consider that, at the time of printing this book, United charged as much as $463 for a one-way ticket from Seattle to New York, while a round-trip ticket could be had for as little as $198.

Be smart. Get a travel agent. Besides, you can't beat the price.

If you like to use the Internet, several travel agents provide similar services, such as finding low fares, without human intervention. Two sites that are especially useful are: www.travelocity.com and www.expedia.com.

2. BOOK THE INITIAL PLANE RESERVATION WITH A MAY OR JUNE RETURN.

The problem with plane reservations is that, when you make your initial jaunt to the campus, you probably will not know when your first finals will be completed. Final exams usually last a week; you might finish them in the first two days or have a final on the very last day. In addition, you may not know if you will be coming home for Thanksgiving break. Needless to say, a lot of things are "iffy."

The problem with "iffy" is that the airlines couldn't care less about your scheduling problems. The cheapest fares are nonrefundable and designed for those who know the exact date of their arrival and departure.

Therefore, you should book the return flight of your first round-trip ticket for the last day of finals at the end of the school year in May or June. All other reservations can be made when you are more in control of your plans. Even if you finish your finals early in May or June, you can spend the last days of your freshman year packing and/or partying.

3. ALWAYS MAKE YOUR RETURN RESERVATION FOR THE LATEST POSSIBLE DATE.

As previously mentioned, you may have trouble finding out when your finals are over. If you discover you are able to leave earlier than expected and possess a ticket with a future date, go on standby and try to grab a vacant seat. Although the rules on most tickets say you cannot employ this tactic, an airline's policy seems to be at the discretion of the gate agent. A kind one may take pity and let you on the flight.

However, no gate agent will let you go standby if the date on your return ticket has come and gone. Thus, make your return reservation for the latest possible date. If worse comes to worst, you stay an extra day or two.

4. SIGN UP FOR FREQUENT-FLIER PROGRAMS.

66 *Traveling from Seattle to Williamstown, it makes real sense to use the frequent-flier programs. When you are traveling that far and paying that much for tickets, you have to do everything possible to defray the cost. Using the frequent-flier programs is the simplest way to make the airlines work for you."*

—Greg Hart, Williams College

Most airlines have frequent-flier programs to encourage you to use the same carrier each time you fly. After flying a certain number of miles, you earn a free flight. Sign up with every airline you use.

Be certain to give your travel agent a mileage number when you book the reservation. Check again at the gate to make sure the mileage number has been entered into the computer.

Many airlines have joined forces with bank credit cards such as VISA and MasterCard, offering frequent-flier miles for money charged to specific credit cards.

Airlines have different mileage requirements to qualify for free trips and/or upgrades. Many airlines work in conjunction with each other. For example, you can use Alaska Air miles on American Airlines, British Airways, Continental Airlines, Hawaiian Airlines, Horizon Air, KLM, Lan Chile, Northwest, or Qantas.

5. CHARGE YOUR AIRLINE TICKETS TO YOUR BANK CARD, IF YOU HAVE ONE.

What difference does it make how you pay for your ticket? Right? Wrong.

Many bank cards give automatic insurance against lost luggage. Those who have lost suitcases realize the significance of this type of insurance. You have a small fortune locked up in those bags. Be shrewd and, if possible, charge your ticket to a bank card.

By the way, don't send your valuable jewelry or irreplaceable computer disks in the suitcases. Carry valuables on board.

 Psst . . . If your luggage has been damaged on the flight, the airline is responsible. Make sure the airline takes care of all repairs.

6. OFFER TO BE BUMPED AND EARN A FREE ROUND-TRIP TICKET.

As a happy-go-lucky college student, it is often wise to give up your seat if the plane is oversold. Not only do you keep your primary ticket, but you might also receive a free round-trip ticket or cash. Free tickets have fewer restrictions and allow ticket holders to change arrival and departure dates without penalty. Open-return tickets like this are a godsend for students with unknown finals schedules.

If you are going to give up your seat, plan on waiting anywhere from 30 minutes to a full day. The airlines will feed you while you are waiting and even pay for a hotel room overnight, if the need arises. Carriers regularly oversell their flights, especially during holidays.

7. WATCH NEWSPAPERS AND THE INTERNET FOR SPECIAL FARES.

When airlines open new routes, they often offer special low fares as incentives. Financially troubled airlines use special rates to lure business. Sometimes the competition follows suit and extends similar fares. Check the newspapers and the Internet for these special bargains. Name your own price travel web sites like www.priceline.com are also a great source for bargains, but only if you have a completely flexible schedule.

Try to be on top of these special prices and book early. Most of the time, an airline will not sell all the seats at a special rate. If you want to be among the lucky ones, don't wait for your travel agent to give you the scoop. He or she may be busy with other clients. Book it yourself.

8. DON'T LOSE YOUR TICKET! GET AN E-TICKET!

The easiest way to ensure that you don't lose your ticket is not to get one in the first place. Electronic Ticketing, or E-Tix, is a system that many airlines are using these days. Passengers may opt to have an e-ticket instead of a paper one, in which case the passenger's ticket is stored in the airline's computer system. Then all the passenger has to do is present identification and sometimes a credit card at the check-in counter. If you are worried about misplacing your ticket, ask for an e-ticket the next time you book a flight.

If you decide to go the old-fashioned, paper-ticket route, then put the return portion of your ticket in a safe place once you arrive on campus. If you lose your ticket, the airlines will ask you to fill out a lost-ticket application and charge you $100—a rather hefty fee—to process the form. The airlines will then make you pay the full price for another ticket. If it is found that your lost ticket was not used by another person, the airlines will refund the price of the ticket, but not the $100.

Those holding "free" tickets (such as tickets earned through the frequent-flier programs) need to be especially careful. If you lose one of these, the airline will not refund you a penny, and you will need to purchase an entirely new ticket.

 Psst . . . The best way to keep your airline ticket is to think of it as cash. You wouldn't crumple up a $100 bill and throw it under a pile of garbage. You wouldn't leave a Ben Franklin lying unattended on your dorm room floor. You would put the money in a safe place for later use. Treat your ticket with similar care.

9. TRY TO TRAVEL LIGHT

In light of world events, airport security is more stringent and time consuming. Put as much as stuff as possible into your checked baggage. You don't want to be waiting in security lines for hours with really heavy carry-on bags. You should strongly consider shipping heavy items like books; lugging that kind of stuff through the airport and around campus while looking for your room is a nightmare. If you insist on bringing certain heavy items in your carry-on, at least make sure it has wheels!

CHAPTER 5

Cars: Driving To and Around Campus

66 *I was driving back to Pomona with my girlfriend to start winter quarter. We thought the car was in good shape, so we just took off without checking the transmission fluid or getting oil or any of that stuff.*

Halfway through the trip, she wakes me up and says, 'David, I think the car sounds funny.' Of course, we are now in the middle of some mountain pass in the boonies of Northern California.

We pulled in at the nearest local service station. Here I am, looking like I just walked out of a J. Crew catalogue, totally at the mercy of some local mechanic who probably hadn't had any major business since World War II.

I'm sure we ended up paying twice what it cost for transmission fluid and an oil change. Needless to say, I now check my car completely before taking a long journey."

—David Muscatel, Pomona College

Is Your Car Going to Make It?

If you are driving to school, be realistic about the condition of your car. Don't play Russian Roulette with a loaded vehicle.

For students whose school is visible from their bedroom, little car preparation is needed, assuming the car runs.

If your school is more than one state away (or on the other side of Texas), make sure your automobile is ready for the journey. The following should be in order:

- ❏ All electrical devices
- ❏ Charged battery
- ❏ Correctly pressured tires and a spare
- ❏ First-aid equipment
- ❏ Flares
- ❏ Functional windshield-wiper blades
- ❏ Sufficient windshield-wiper fluid
- ❏ Jack
- ❏ Jumper cables
- ❏ New oil and filter
- ❏ Sufficient radiator fluid
- ❏ Sufficient brake fluid
- ❏ Tool kit

Instead of trying to check all the important fluids yourself, many recommend taking the car into a Jiffy Lube or a similar car maintenance establishment. These shops will check and change your oil, filter, transmission fluid, brake fluid, windshield-wiper wash, radiator fluid, water, and differential fluid. The cost of the service is around $30, and cheap for the peace of mind that comes from knowing your car is not going to run out of brake fluid in the middle of nowhere.

Regardless of whether you do it yourself or have it done professionally, you should change your oil about every 3000 miles.

 Psst . . . It is definitely a good idea to get all the problems with your car taken care of before leaving for college. If your brakes are faulty or your taillight is broken, take your car to a shop in your hometown. Car problems are the last thing you will want to worry about once at college.

Joining a Motor Club and Planning a Route

For long journeys, consult a motor club for a route plan. Although smaller motor companies like Allstate Motor Club offer similar services, the American Automobile Association (AAA, pronounced "Triple-A") is the largest and most extensive. If you are not a member of one of these clubs, consider joining before venturing to school.

Members of AAA receive Triptiks, maps, tourbooks, and travelers checks— free of charge. A Triptik is a comprehensive, day-by-day guide of how to get where you are going. You can prepare a Triptik with an AAA employee a week before your journey.

More importantly, if your car gets stuck on the way, motor clubs come at the ring of a telephone and tow you to safety. For no charge, AAA will tow your car up to 10 miles. After 10 miles, you pay a slight towing fee, but that's better than being at the mercy of an independent towing company that wants cash and lots of it. (If your trip to school takes you across vast, uninhabited areas, AAA also offers a Plus membership that, among other benefits, extends your free towing limit to 100 miles.)

Don't take a chance, especially if you're going to be driving long distances— join a club.

Some Don'ts of Driving Your Car to School

1. DON'T DRIVE ALONE.

Unless you have a short drive, don't risk driving alone. Another person can keep you company—and awake at the wheel.

2. DON'T DRIVE AT NIGHT.

Nighttime means different things to different people. To long-distance drivers, it signifies more accidents. Follow the 8 A.M. to 8 P.M. rule recommended by AAA. Twelve hours of driving is plenty! And be sure to stop every couple of hours for a short break—maybe to grab a bite to eat or to take a bathroom break.

3. DON'T WAIT UNTIL THE "NIGHT OF" TO CALL A MOTEL.

If possible, make reservations at a motel the day before you arrive in a city. Driving around unknown city streets looking for accommodations is not productive. Many towns will not have motels with available rooms.

4. DON'T CARRY TOO MUCH CASH.

Cash may be king, but you are a joker if you carry too much. Traveler's checks and credit cards are safer.

5. DON'T LEAVE ANYTHING VALUABLE IN YOUR CAR.

Holy Toledo! Don't fall to the same fate as the protagonist in the following story. He left his clothes in the back seat of his car. If you want to keep it, lock your stuff in the trunk or take it with you wherever you go.

❝ *It was the first leg of my journey home from Cornell. Toledo, Ohio was our first overnight stop. We checked in and brought our valuables into the room—stereo, tapes and compact discs.*

Yet, for some reason, Mr. Justification, that awful demon inside my head, convinced me that I could leave my large blue duffel bag with all my wardrobe in the back seat of the car. I am a short boy—a short, stocky boy. 'Who would want my clothes? Who would wear my clothes?' I thought.

Obviously, there must be some short, stocky derelict running around out there because the next morning my blue duffel bag was gone. From now on, I don't leave anything in the car."

—David Stern, Cornell University

6. DON'T DRIVE IN INCLEMENT WEATHER.

If you are driving on the West Coast, this might not be a problem. Otherwise, be careful when Mother Nature starts playing hardball.

During heavy showers, sleet, or snow, pull over and wait it out. Don't ask for trouble. As University of Washington student Skip Slavin warned, "Smaller cars tend to hydroplane in four inches of Pacific Northwest rain."

7. DON'T SPEED . . . BIG BROTHER IN BLACK AND WHITE IS WATCHING!

The speed limit on most interstate highways has been raised to 65, and even 75 on some highways. Hopefully, that's high enough to keep most of you closet racecar drivers happy.

If you drive more than 10 miles per hour over the limit for any length of time, plan on being stopped. Interstates are full of cops ready to catch speeders, especially speeders from out of state. You don't want to start off your college career with a speeding ticket, so keep your eyes peeled for speed limit signs and don't push your luck.

 Psst . . . Speeding tickets play havoc with your insurance rates, which are probably high enough already.

8. BRING SOME GOOD CDS OR BOOKS ON TAPE.

Good music can make a long car ride seem much shorter. So can a decent book on tape. If you can't afford new CDs/tapes, borrow from your friends and send them back when you arrive.

Tips after Arrival

You made it to school. Your car is intact. Great! Or is it? Having a car on campus can be a nightmare.

❝ *However pathetic it sounds, the day mom told me I could take her car to school was one of the happiest moments of my life. Now I could drive for late-night munchies whenever I wanted. I could go to the city on weekends. I could impress women with my rough-and-tumble, four-door Toyota Camry—I wish?*

I was psyched. That is, I was psyched until the car's transmission blew. Nirvana became hell in a hurry. After calling home several hundred times, visiting 20-some odd transmission dealers, and wasting approximately four full days trying to find the best deal, I was forced to shell out $2,800 to Mr. Aamco for a new transmission. Two days later, my muffler broke. But that's another story.

I'm not saying having a car at school isn't great. But sometimes it can be more trouble than it's worth.❞

—Greg Gottesman, Stanford University

1. HAVE A SET OF JUMPER CABLES HANDY AT ALL TIMES.

Forgetting to turn off your lights saps juice from a battery. Jumper cables can save you from sure disaster.

If you are located in an especially cold region, start your car every day and let it run a few minutes. Five or six days of dormancy kills a battery, especially in cold weather.

Note that if you are an AAA member, you can call their toll-free number for roadside assistance, and a tow truck will come and "jump" your dead battery for free (the fee is covered as part of your membership fee). Yet another reason to sign up for AAA.

2. BE CAREFUL WHERE YOU PARK AT SCHOOL.

Meter maids can be nasty on college campuses. Most schools allow you to buy parking passes for campus lots. Often the fee is high, but the cost of several parking tickets is higher.

Parking on streets is usually impossible, unless you are blessed with incredible luck.

66 *Parking at the University of Washington is a joke. I literally would skip appointments and not go places just to keep a good spot. It sounds ludicrous, but when you spend an hour and a half one night looking for an opening, you start to cherish a good parking space.*

I remember my mom asking me if I wanted to drive home for a home-cooked meal once and telling her, 'Mom, I know this sounds incredibly stupid, but, if I come home, I am going to lose my parking spot in front of the frat house.' It got so bad that I just started keeping my car at home."

—Dan Gottesman, University of Washington

3. SET A POLICY EARLY ON CAR-SHARING.

If you have a car on campus, friends will wish to borrow it. Set some guidelines early so you don't run into problems. For example, you might make a rule that whoever uses the car has to return it with the tank at least as full as when they borrowed it.

Many a friend has wrecked a car, and it's your insurance that pays. Expect a gigantic insurance hike or cancellation if your car is involved in an accident with or without you in it. When at all possible, drive your friends where they need to go, instead of just dishing out the keys.

> 66 *I let my roommate borrow my car. It was one of those things where her car broke down at the last minute, so I felt kind of bad for her. The next thing I know, I get a call from the police telling me my car is completely totaled. My roommate was fine, but after the accident, she never offered to buy me a new car or even a fender. Now, the only thing I can use my car for is used parts. Next time I will definitely think twice about lending out my car so easily."*
>
> —Cynthia Twiss, Washington State University

4. LOCK YOUR DOORS AND TAKE YOUR RADIO INSIDE.

Don't get too attached to that expensive radio in the car. Thousands get stolen each year. If you have a removable car stereo, don't put it in the trunk; that's the first place crooks look. Store it in your room.

Remember thieves thrive on college campuses. Play it safe and always lock your car doors.

5. PROTECT YOUR CAR

College campuses are havens for car thieves. Car alarms or even fake car alarms are great deterrents. Steering wheel locks also keep away unwanted intruders. Remember that thieves would rather spend time on easy pickings.

Do You Really Need a Car?

Before you drive to school, you must ask yourself: Do I need a car?

Remember that, at most schools, you cannot drive to class; there is either no parking or the classrooms are situated where there are no roads.

Rising insurance rates, having the responsibility of being a chauffeur, being constantly pestered by friends who want to borrow your car, parking, and maintaining the health of your four-wheeler are all problems automobile owners must consider.

Plus, most campuses are pretty self-contained, and it is not uncommon for college students to find that they never really have to leave campus. Everything is right there, or at least within a short walk. And if your school is located somewhere that has a good public transportation system, then hopping on a bus might turn out to be a heck of a lot easier than dealing with the hassles of owning a car.

66 *Most people want a car when they go to college. After driving in high school, they're accustomed to the freedom and independence of being able to drive. But I didn't really think I needed a car when I went to college. The hassle of people asking me to borrow it, parking, gas money, repairs, insurance . . . I just thought college would give me enough to worry about.*

Also, late-night Denny's stops can become costly, but having to ride your bike to the Denny's off campus will dissuade even a Grand Slam Breakfast fanatic from going too often. Of course, this is not to mention the fact that my parents said I absolutely, positively could not have a car.

After my first few quarters, I have decided that I really don't need one. If I am in dire need, I can always find a ride. Plus, college has everything I need right on campus—books, toothpaste, hospital, women."

—Joseph Elford, Stanford University

CHAPTER 6

Orientation

66 *My plane was scheduled to leave for Detroit Metro Airport from Newark at about 4 P.M. I was on my way to a three-day summer orientation program at the University of Michigan in Ann Arbor.*

Unfortunately, complications arose as soon as I walked up to the gate to receive a seat assignment. The woman at the terminal told me—get this!—'The runways are too hot, so we will have to cancel flight 293.'

'The runways are too hot?' I thought. 'You have got to be kidding me.'

Luckily, I met two girls who happened to be going to orientation as well. We talked for about an hour and found out we had some common acquaintances. When we finally got on a plane to Detroit, the pilot gave us some more bad news. 'Due to bad weather in Detroit, we've been diverted to Cleveland.'

'Cleveland!' we all said in disbelief. 'This is getting ridiculous.'

By the time we got to Michigan, it was 5 A.M. Orientation was to begin in three hours.

Even though I probably should have been upset about the airplane fiasco and all, I wasn't. Twelve hours ago I had been terrified of college. Since then I had made some new friends and come to the conclusion that things could only go up from here."

—Andy Gottesman, University of Michigan

Five Tips for Orientation

For many, orientation week turns out to be the best part of freshman year. No homework. No parents. New environment. New friends. Parties. Parties. More parties.

Besides the fun and games, you will be registering for classes (See Chapter 8, "Choosing Classes"), taking placement exams, and finding out where you fit into your new home. Here are five tips to help make your orientation experience more fun—and hopefully more fruitful as well.

 Psst . . . Not all schools have the same type of orientation. Some may be three days, others a week. Some might be during the middle of summer, others right before school starts. In addition, the orientation activities will be different at each college.

1. GET OUT AND MEET AS MANY PEOPLE AS POSSIBLE!

66 *I had a friend who decided to stay in her assigned dorm room for most of the orientation. When she came back to school in the fall, she was disappointed because it seemed that everyone else had more friends than she did. She told me that missing the 'initial' meeting period during orientation had left her feeling out of place at college.*

'I'm still being introduced to people that my friends are already acquainted with,' she said. 'I should have made more of an effort during orientation."

—Frances Carhart, Wellesley College

Orientation is perhaps the only time when nearly all outside pressures are placed on hold. You won't have any homework or jobs to think about. Take advantage of this and try to make as many new friends as possible. Remember that everyone is in the same boat—a new environment, new group of people, new school—and everyone will be as eager to meet you as you are to meet them.

Don't be afraid to initiate contact with someone you don't know. "Hi, I'm Hugh, from Duluth . . ." is always a good way to start (especially if your name is Hugh!), but it doesn't really matter what you say, people will be wanting to talk, and a simple question like "Are you heading to the dining hall?" may end up as the start of a conversation with your new best friend.

Don't just hang out with the people you already know from high school. Don't ignore them either, but spread out . . . lest you meet the same fate as the protagonist in the following story.

66 *My friend from home and I stuck together like glue during orientation. We missed home and wanted to stay together.*

But hanging out so much at orientation was a bad idea because when we came back in September a lot of other students were always saying, 'Oh, you were in my orientation group . . . what's up?' They had built up some sort of foundation already for getting to know new people at school.

Looking back on it, I wish I had done more of that."

—Shari Solomon, University of Vermont

2. EXPLORE YOUR NEW DIGS.

One of the best things to do once you arrive on campus is to gather up some new acquaintances and take your own personal tour of the campus and the surrounding city.

A guided tour will give you only a superficial look at the place you will be spending the next four years. When you go on your own exploration, look for the "grease spots" and unique eateries. These may come in handy later in the fall as alternatives to university food service. If you can, ask some older students which are the best places to visit. They usually have a pretty good idea of where students hang out.

Also check out the location of other "necessities," such as the post office, your laundry facilities, public transportation services, and, of course, convenience stores.

3. SAMPLE THE NIGHT LIFE AT YOUR COLLEGE.

Whatever you do, don't lock yourself in your room. Much of college is social, and it would be a shame to ignore that reality during your orientation.

Experiment. Go to a Greek party, even if you don't plan on rushing. Grab a group of newfound friends and sample a local pub in town, or go out dancing. Have a blast.

4. ATTEND A FEW WORKSHOPS AND TAKE THE NECESSARY EXAMS.

Your orientation pamphlet undoubtedly will be filled with activities and lectures, which could take up your entire day.

Some of these workshops and lectures may prove worthwhile, but it would be a mistake to try to attend every one at the expense of not meeting people. Go to the lectures that seem to be the most interesting, and don't worry about the rest. Trust us, it won't affect your grades down the road.

In addition, don't forget to take the necessary placement exams in math, English, foreign languages, chemistry, and the like. If you plan on taking upper-level courses, some schools require you to pass the placement tests in these areas. Should you study for these exams? Not really. Just give it your best shot, and you'll probably end up where you belong.

5. HAVE FUN . . . ORIENTATION COMES ONLY ONCE.

It's that simple. Orientation is not a time to worry about classes (except when you are signing up for them) or homework or anything for that matter. It's a time to get a quick glance at your new home and the people that will be living there. Enjoy it. It comes only once.

CHAPTER 7

Roommates

“ *I'm temporarily falling quite out of love with life, Boston University, and my roommate. Since we've been living with each other inseparably for two months, we're picking up each other's expressions, finishing each other's sentences, and arguing more and more. It's starting to get to me.*

Of late, the scenario is:

> *'Can I borrow your computer?'*
>
> *'TAKE it!'*
>
> *'Why does everything offend you lately?'*
>
> *'I'm not offended. I'm trying to STUDY.'*
>
> *'Why don't you go to the lounge?'*
>
> *'Because I want to study here.'*
>
> *'Well, fine.'*
>
> *'FINE!' (Door slams)*

Approximate time until next confrontation: Seven minutes. I still adore her, though. I guess I do . . . usually. I mean how couldn't you adore someone you eat, sleep, shower, study, and breathe with 24 hours a day?”

—Samantha Grey, Boston University

Your New Companion

Many schools ask you to fill out a form describing your own living habits during the summer before you get to school. In theory, this form is used to match you with compatible roommates, so this can be a valuable tool for you if you know how to use it right.

The first thing to remember is BE HONEST; don't say that you enjoy lifting weights for two hours every morning at 5 A.M. if by "every morning" you mean that you lifted weights once during your junior year of high school. Also, don't say that you want your room to be party central if you are really more of a mild partier. The people in the housing office at school are not evaluating you on "coolness"; basically they couldn't care less if you like to go to bed at 5 A.M. every night. But they will be using everything you say to match you with your roommate.

One of the best ways to think of it is that on a roommate information form, you should describe not yourself, but the person that you think you would most like to live with. Obviously that does not mean that you should falsify your form, but if you are going to err, err toward describing your ideal living partner, not your idea of coolness.

Those with brothers or sisters know that living with peers takes compromise and effort. Multiply the factor by five when you throw two people from disparate backgrounds into the same room!

Roommate Rules: Everyday Etiquette

The good news is that your future roommate(s) is as overwhelmed and unsure about college as you are. Both of you will come to college—labels and titles you bore in high school defunct—forced to face hundreds of new challenges. While no one will ever say you and your roommate have to be best friends, a congenial living situation makes freshman year easier—and more fun.

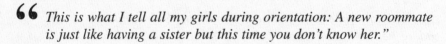 *This is what I tell all my girls during orientation: A new roommate is just like having a sister but this time you don't know her."*

—Resident Advisor Shiela Wilson, Bloomsburgh University

Here are a few rules of etiquette to help you along the way.

1. GET IN TOUCH BEFORE SCHOOL STARTS.

Confront your nervousness and curiosity by contacting your roommate before school. A phone call will serve as a stress-reducer and give you a chance to coordinate belongings. Who's bringing the stereo? What about the telephone and answering machine? Do you need two hair dryers?

Hopefully, as you are arranging details, some common interests will surface. If you learn that he was the high school quarterback, while you were president of the Physics Club, don't panic. In a few weeks, you will enter school as two individuals with something very much in common . . . frosh status or, in simpler terms, no status.

 Psst . . . Many schools do not release roommate names before school. In this case, you just have to wait until you arrive at school.

2. DON'T JUMP TO CONCLUSIONS.

The first glimpse you will get of your roommate may be amidst a collage of parents, siblings, and suitcases—pure chaos. Hold back judgments. Saying good-bye to relatives can be sad or embarrassing, depending upon the person.

Don't catch First Impression Syndrome (FIS); it kills enough friendships already.

Remember that going to college is a new experience for every freshman and will be the cause of anxiety for many people.

3. PRIORITIZE STUDY HOURS.

Much like fingerprints, everyone's study habits are different. If you need silence for studying while your roommate cannot comprehend calculus without the Grateful Dead, negotiate evenings that you will trade going to the library or study lounge.

Compromise! Ask for quiet hours after 10 P.M. or offer your Walkman. Budget your time so you do not pull all-nighters that keep both of you awake.

4. NEGOTIATE EARLY . . . START WITH THE PHONE BILL.

Voice your concerns early. Do you have pet peeves? Do you hate people who leave toenail clippings on the floor? It's easier to listen and compromise in the beginning of the year than two months into the semester.

Start with the telephone bill. Since one person probably has agreed to have the bill charged to his or her name, discuss payment procedures for the other person involved. How do you want to be paid? Cash or check? Do you want the money before sending in the bill?

While you are at it, air other reservations you have. What would be your reaction to your roommate's friend calling at 2 A.M.? Do you hate people who don't take complete phone messages? Do you like onions but not olives on your pizza?

66 *During sophomore year, my friend had a roommate who would al-ways squirm his way out of paying his equal share.*

For example, when we would order from Domino's, he would always volunteer to pay the delivery man. There would be three of us, and he would ask us each for a five spot. The problem was, the pizza only cost 11 bucks. He would then chip in his one dollar and eat about half the pie.

With the phone bill, he would only add in his long-distance calls and never pay his part of the local charges. My friend, who had to pay the rest of the bill, wanted to kill the guy.

With beer, he was even worse. He would only pay about half of what we did and then finish off three-fourths of the case.

My friend felt too cheap to bring it up, so he never did. I didn't either. It bugged us the whole year.

In the end, I wish we would have confronted him early in the year and talked to him about how he could have been a better roommate and friend. Other than having a tight wallet, he actually was one of the cooler guys at school. I'm sure he could have been a much better roommate and friend had we simply told him he wasn't being fair and negotiated the problem when it first came up."

—Beau Brown, Pierce Community College

5. RESPECT R.E.M. (NOT THE GROUP!)

Any Don Quixote can tell you that messing with your roommate's sleep is the last—the very last—thing you want to do. In simpler terms, don't bring your buddies in to watch David Letterman when your roommate is taking a siesta. Don't slam doors or drawers at 8:20 A.M. (Yes, 8:20 A.M. is very, very early in college!) Don't type a term paper till dawn when you know your roommate needs sleep. Don't study at night with the overhead light on when a desk lamp will suffice.

66 *Blessings on him who first invented sleep. It covers a man all over, thoughts and all, like a cloak. It is meat for the hungry, drink for the thirsty, heat for the cold, and cold for the hot. It makes the shepherd equal to the monarch, and the fool to the wise."*

—Miguel de Cervantes, Don Quixote

6. LIMIT OVERNIGHT GUESTS.

Be as flexible as possible with this one.

If your roommate has guests from home or other universities, offer to spend the night in a neighbor's room. Of course, if the visitor is staying more than a few nights, explaining that he or she needs to bring a sleeping bag is more than acceptable. If you are planning to have guests, it's best to let your roommate know as far ahead of time as possible.

66 *My roommate, Amit, has been planning all year long to perform in a South Asian dance show called Gungharoo. He planned the choreography, planned the publicity, and organized the ticket sales. However, unbeknownst to his nine roommates, he has also been planning for 15 of his closest friends from home to come and live with us. I say 'live' because there can be no 'visit' once the four-day visitor's permit has expired. So 15 people have come to spend their Spring Break in our room, and since they wouldn't want to be deprived of a fun break, they have naturally turned the room into quite a party zone.*

The fact that we have midterms has been but a minor irritation because basically we're hospitable guys. Sneaking 15 people into the dining hall isn't easy, and neither is sleeping when 5 A.M. constitutes only the beginning of the end of their night. But, as I said, we're hospitable guys, so it's cool. Yesterday we played basketball, and upon returning the pack began to call first shower, second shower, etc. Before I knew it, I was stuck with the sixteenth shower in my own room, and that feeling of hospitality had started to fade somewhat. Then we tried to play Trivial Pursuit. But with two teams and 25 people, Trivial Pursuit is like a giant model UN conference . . . 95 percent haggling and 5 percent action. And as the days go by, I yearn for the days when I could walk out in the common room and talk to my girlfriend on the phone without worrying about waking someone up at 1 P.M."

—Bryan Leach, Harvard University

If you are the one with guests, make sure not to take advantage of the room. It's not just "yours."

Psst . . . Overnight guests of the opposite sex present a special problem. This topic, often raising moral issues, should be discussed immediately and openly. Respect each other's opinions and define policy clearly. Better to confront embarrassing situations before they arise rather than at 2 A.M. when you walk into a setting tailored for a Michelangelo painting.

7. DEFINE PROPERTY RIGHTS.

❝ *During my first semester, I had a 4 P.M. psychology class. At various times during the week, my roommate would get home from an earlier class and change into my clothes. To make matters worse, she then would scurry off to a happy hour somewhere on campus.*

Later in the night, I would run into her at an ATO or SAE party. She would greet me with an alcohol-induced smile and say, 'By the way, thanks for the outfit . . . you know how well this color goes with my eyes.' The statement would come at about the same time some guy would bump into her and spill beer all over my sweater. I wanted to shoot her.

The thing is, I was paying for being glib and dishonest the first week
of school when I said, 'Oh sure, borrow anything . . . really, I don't
mind.' I never thought she would take me up on it—daily."

—Jessica Hall, Syracuse University

Most college students do not mind sharing umbrellas, lending a few tapes, or spotting for a movie. Monopolizing a wardrobe or another's pocketbook is a whole different ball game.

While you and your sister may have traded sweaters like baseball cards, your roommate might cringe every time you venture toward her favorite cardigan.

Don't allow the simple niceties of asking before borrowing to fade as you become more familiar with your roommate. Respect your roommate's right to say no.

If you do borrow something from your roommate and end up losing it or damaging it, an immediate replacement is not only courteous, but will also minimize resentment!

8. CLEANING: KEEP YOUR END OF THE BARGAIN.

Discovering an immaculate college dorm room in October and your breaking Barry Bonds' home run record share similar odds in Las Vegas. The speed of light to one, to be exact!

If you are used to starched sheets, forget it. Learn to tolerate a roommate's unmade bed. But just because you are discarding delusions of *House Beautiful* does not mean you should accept or create conditions that are unhealthy and/ or unlivable.

Most importantly, be considerate. Don't let your wet towel mold on top of your roommate's desk—or yours, for that matter. If she asks you to remove the stale tuna salad from the refrigerator, don't argue . . . do it!

Lead by example. If you want to live in unblemished paradise, clean your side of the room and hope your roommate follows suit. Occasionally, you can even start the job for the loafer.

9. EXPECT NORMAL TENSIONS.

Even the best roommate situations can turn ugly. When everything bugs you—the way she brushes her teeth, flosses, combs her hair, flirts, applies too much eyeliner, and tries on seventeen different outfits checking for fat rolls on her 97-pound body—RELAX! Don't turn your roommate into a scapegoat or a permanent punching bag. No one wants you to take the place of mom.

Take disagreements or conflicts in stride and try to get away from the room for a while. Finally, be tolerant, especially if your roommate has had a bad day.

Remember that unlike your other friends, you have to live with your roommate, so if at all possible you will want to avoid "blowing up" at your roommate when you get upset. Try to stay calm and just get some space. Remember that there is some truth to the old adage that "sugar works better than spice."

10. STOP RUMORS BY NOT STARTING THEM.

66 *It seemed wherever I went first semester, I heard private conversations among four or five girls who obsessively attacked vulnerable aspects of their roommates. They drew pictures, reminiscent of elementary school squabbles, and gossiped until silenced by the entrance of the innocent victim.*

They would say things like, 'Every time her boyfriend calls, even if she is already asleep, she'll jump out of bed and rush to see him. She has no mind of her own.'

Meanwhile, the oblivious roommate only heard rumors and received unjustified glares."

—Katie Sapadin, Emory University

Don't volunteer the details of your roommate's life to the rest of the dorm, fraternity, or sorority. Weekly floor meetings should not serve as a gossip central, where the main agenda item is who owes $50 for a 93-minute phone call to the boyfriend at home. Remember . . . trust, once violated, is impossible to regain.

11. TAKE ADVANTAGE OF, NOT OFFENSE TO, YOUR ROOMMATE'S CHOICE OF CHUMS.

During the first week of college, roommates tend to cling together. As the year progresses and your circle of friends multiplies, however, you may choose to socialize less and less.

Neither of you is responsible for the other's social life; personality differences undoubtedly will cause you to prefer different friends.

Instead of resenting your roommate for his selection of buddies, take advantage of it. Through each other, you can gain greater access to a network of people, cultures, ideas, and opportunities. The acquaintances you make through your roommate can only add to your college experience.

12. THEY DON'T HAVE TO BE YOUR BEST FRIENDS.

Roommates, like brothers or sisters, can become best friends—but they don't have to be. Aim for congeniality. If anything more develops, that's an extra bonus. Remember that living with someone else is very difficult, no matter who it is. It involves daily compromise and a lot of accommodating the other person's habits.

 My freshman year I was in a room with four guys. My first impression was that Jacob seemed to be the one who was most similar to me; in fact, I couldn't figure out how I got assigned to live with the other two guys.

Jake and I are similar, in some ways, but it wasn't long before we found our differences. In October, we started a discussion about politics at dinner and ended up arguing about whether janitors and lawyers deserved the same pay or not. Jake wouldn't talk to me for a couple days after that. He thought I was a capitalist pig, and I thought he was a communist idealist.

Then we began to discover other fissures—Jake likes to have his own private space, and he is very neat. I am a 'what's mine is yours' guy, and, well, I'm not neat to say the least.

By about half way through the year it was clear that Jake and I were not meant to live together. But the funny thing is, we had developed a very close friendship. During our sophomore year we didn't live together, but we stayed close, and whenever one of us was down and out, we always relied on the other.

It's too bad that we couldn't live together, but I'm glad we got assigned to each other freshman year because I gained one of my closest, wisest friends out of the experience."

—Daniel Baer, Harvard University

Sometimes you will find that you like your roommate a lot, but just have trouble living with him or her. That's normal too; just do your best to get through the year and keep up the friendship.

13. IF EVERYTHING ELSE FAILS, CALL IN A MEDIATOR.

You have begged your roommate to stop leaving underwear on the floor. You have discussed it calmly and not so calmly. War looks inevitable.

Don't be afraid to call in a dorm counselor or a trusted friend of both parties when you and your roommate face an unpleasant stalemate.

Vocalizing the problem with an outsider may help both of you deal with the dilemma in a more constructive and less personal way. The mediator often will see obvious solutions that may never cross a miffed mind.

If both of you are still unwilling to compromise, ask the mediator to make the decision for you. Of course, both sides will have to abide by the ruling, regardless of who gets the short end of the deal.

❝ *To some, I had the perfect roommate situation. We both studied a lot, were neat, had early morning classes, and could sleep with the light on. What more could you want? But what seemed perfect could hardly be called that. My roommate and I had a bland, almost businesslike relationship. The only way I could describe her to my family was 'like a bug in your soup—she doesn't take up much room.'*

While I was constantly rambling on about my day or my classes, she would merely listen and never reciprocate with a similar anecdote. Eventually, I stopped rambling, and together we redefined the word 'silence.'

Our conversation upon returning from winter break consisted of:

'How was it?'

'Fine.'

*It wasn't until March that she felt comfortable enough with me to
share stories. We learned more about each other in the final two
months than we had all year. A little late perhaps, but we finally
became friends."*

—Jessica Hall, Syracuse University

14. ALLOW TIME TO DEVELOP A REAL FRIENDSHIP.

When befriending another person, sharing part of yourself proves crucial to a
genuine bond. Although you may enjoy eating meals together or studying as a
pair, no real friendship can progress beyond small talk unless both participants
open up. It takes some people more time to do this than others. Be patient.

Speak honestly about your experiences and accomplishments. False displays
of grandeur are unnecessary and unwelcome.

Just as important, be a good listener. It's no coincidence that listeners have
more "true" friends than talkers.

15. BE YOURSELF.

You shouldn't try to change your roommate, and he or she shouldn't try to
change you. Why? Because:

1. Individuality is something to be admired, not frowned upon.

2. Changing people never works anyway.

If you do nothing else throughout your college years, be yourself and allow
others that right. This doesn't mean you shouldn't try to grow and become a
better person. However, playing games and pretending to be "who you are not"
only leads to unforeseen problems and low self-esteem. The odd thing is, more
people will like you for who you are rather than for who you pretend to be.

Be yourself . . . it's not as corny as it sounds.

CHAPTER 8

Choosing Classes

66 *I needed a fourth class, and I was desperate to find one. I thought that a class in the Women's Studies department might be an easy route. I looked at two classes, one was called I Like Ike, I Love Lucy and was about 1950s American culture. The other was called Gender and Class in Jane Austen.*

I had already read almost all of Jane Austen's books in high school, and I figured, hey, how tough can this be. So I went to the class. The professor made it sound like a party—the syllabus looked great—the readings were a bunch of Jane Austen books, no exams, only two papers, and we were going to get together in the evenings to watch all of the movies. Then the professor announced that the first movie we were going to watch was Clueless, and I knew I had found my academic utopia.

But all good things come to an end. The class ended up being bogged down with a lot of heavy historical background material. And on the day that the first paper was to be returned, the professor announced, 'Well, there are 17 people in this class, and six of you got a B– or higher. For those who received Ds and Fs, you may rewrite for partial credit.'

Needless to say, my dream class quickly became a nightmare. Now I know that if a class seems too good to be true, it probably is."

—Alicia Carasquillo, Harvard University

Ten Tips on Choosing Classes

Most high school students didn't get to choose which courses to take. In college, however, selecting your classes will be invaluable in determining what type of education you receive. Here are ten ways to help you choose classes—the right way.

1. DON'T OVERBURDEN YOURSELF.

For most students, the first quarter of freshman year marks a time of adjustment. Every freshman is bombarded with a host of new acquaintances, new activities, and new responsibilities.

For these reasons, overburdening yourself with a gigantic course load is foolish. You will have plenty of time to take many of the classes listed on the time schedule during later semesters.

At the same time, don't take such a light course load that you won't be challenged. Perhaps the best idea, then, is to take an average course load, which amounts to 15 units or credits at most colleges. In this way, you will not seriously overburden yourself, and you will be able to measure how much time you need to study during an average 15-unit semester. Remember that no matter what, you will have less class time in college. The fact that you took 25 hours of classes per week in high school does not mean that you are slacking off by taking 15 per week in college!

 Psst . . . Always take enough units so that, if you drop a course (perhaps one that you are failing), you will not go on academic probation. Many schools put students on academic probation if they take nine units or fewer. Thus, it is a good idea to always sign up for 15 units or more, so you can drop one five-unit class if necessary.

2. DON'T SIGN UP FOR THREE READING-INTENSIVE COURSES.

Try to vary the type of courses you take, especially freshman year. You don't want to be stuck in the library your first week of school with three readers the size of *War and Peace*.

College courses require much more reading than courses in high school—a professor is not being "cruel and unusual" (although he or she may be unreasonable) for assigning 500 pages of reading per week. When you multiply that times four, you get 2,000 pages = no way in heck you are ever leaving the library. By the same token, although a problem set may have only two problems, it could take you four hours of brain teasing to figure it out, and you still might not get the right answer! So try to balance your class load between courses that might have a lot of reading (usually humanities courses) and courses that have problem sets (usually math and sciences).

In terms of specifics, math/science courses would include biology, chemistry, physics, and, of course, calculus, and geometry; these classes will usually have problem sets for homework.

Humanities or reading-intensive courses might include classes in anthropology, English, history, political science, psychology, and various other social sciences.

3. SAMPLE A VARIETY OF SUBJECT AREAS.

❝ *There are many college courses that you will have never even heard of while in high school. Sociology, psychology, political science, communication, art history . . . the list is endless. You will be cheating yourself if you don't try out some of these new areas of study. You know, it's not uncommon for a pre-med to switch to an art history major after finding out that pre-med is boring and art history is his or her true love."*

—Katie MacDonald, University of Washington

As much as it might feel like the people around you have their futures set in definite plans, they don't. Or at least the smart ones don't. If you go to college with your career plans set in stone, you are going to miss out on three-fourths of the "college experience." It's okay to be leaning toward pre-med or political science, but don't rule out other subject areas without giving them a chance.

❝ *My sophomore year I decided to take an Afro-Brazilian dance class just for fun. It was two nights a week and I actually got credit for it. It was probably the best class I've taken so far! I had so much fun every time, and the professor was this totally hilarious guy who jumped around the room. What a blast!"*

—Katie Woo, Tufts University

Subjects you enjoyed in high school may not interest you in college. Besides that, you may find academic nirvana in a totally random subject area. Come to college with an open mind; you can always switch back to your original academic plans at a later date.

If you have your heart set on law school or medical school and think you need to major in a certain area, think again. Law schools, medical schools, and business schools are encouraging students to major in a variety of areas. In other words, you don't need to be an economics major to go to business school. You don't need to be a pre-law major to go to law school. And you don't need to be a biology major to go to medical school; you only need the prerequisites.

4. CHOOSE PROFESSORS, NOT TITLES.

❝ *The biggest mistake people make when choosing classes is looking at the course titles. They'll take a class like 'Abortion and the Supreme Court' or 'Suspense in Alfred Hitchcock' just because it sounds interesting. What students should be more concerned with is the professor who is teaching the class—not the class itself.*

A bad teacher can make the most interesting subject boring. Similarly, a good teacher can make 'Weaving in Ancient Togo' the most fascinating course at college. Ask older students and your advisor who the best teachers are.

Pick exciting professors. You'll end up sleeping through the boring classes anyway."

—Greg Gottesman, Stanford University

As the last anecdote attests, a professor makes a course—not the other way around. Find out who the best professors are and take their classes, especially if they are in your field. Even if they are not in your field, try to get into classes with the best teachers.

 Psst . . . Just because someone is a Nobel laureate does not make him or her a great lecturer or teacher. Sign up for the best teaching professors, not the best researchers.

5. GET YOUR REQUIREMENTS OUT OF THE WAY EARLY.

Most schools have distribution requirements that make it mandatory for each student to take courses in a variety of areas. A great way to sample various fields during your freshman year is to take classes that help fulfill your distribution requirements. University distribution requirements often turn out to be interesting courses, which may lead your education in a totally different direction.

Also, part of your freshman course list should include your school's foreign language requirement. Come the last quarter of senior year, you are not going to want to be sitting in a Spanish class when you have 15 units of your major to complete.

6. TALK WITH OLDER STUDENTS AS WELL AS YOUR ADVISOR.

When choosing classes, you can consult a multitude of people. You probably will be assigned an advisor, whom you will meet with on a regular basis to discuss course plans. The only problem is that these advisors usually do not have a "pulse" on which are the best courses and who are the best teachers.

Older students in your dorm or frat/sorority house will be able to give you more of the "inside scoop" on many of the classes you are considering. They can tell you who are the interesting professors and who are the duds. Ask as many older students as possible. They will be flattered that someone thinks their opinion means something.

66 *After a speech about how our academic advisors would be assigned based on our own interests, I was told that mine was Barry Nailbuff, a professor in the economics department who was also interested in squash.*

I have no interest in either economics or squash.

The next day I met with Barry to discuss the classes I would take first semester and he convinced me to drop my introductory American history course and take Politics 336: Introduction to World Order, taught by Professor Richard Falk.

'Dick and I play squash,' he said.

Taking my advisor's advice, I signed up for the class.

It was the worst experience of my life because no freshman mind could hope to comprehend this course."

—Jim Grossman, Princeton University

Your advisor and your parents are better suited to deal with your long-term plans, not your immediate course selection.

7. DON'T GET FRUSTRATED IF CLASSES ARE CLOSED.

Despite what other students may say, you usually can get into a course if you are willing to persevere and sit in on the first few class sessions. This, of course, does not include the smaller seminars, which often are reserved for juniors, seniors, and graduate students. But large lecture courses tend to let everybody in—eventually. What's one extra body?

If there is a course that you really want to take, don't be afraid to call the professor or the head teaching assistant (TA) at the department office. Say something like "I know the class is full, but I really was looking forward to taking it and if there's anything you can do to squeeze me in, I would really appreciate it." Nine times out of 10, you'll get in.

❝ *Registration isn't always so easy. While I was registering for winter-term classes, I got to the registration room only to find a line about 50 people deep. My registration date was the last one at the university, so I'd listed about twice the number of classes I needed.*

I got one—'Great Books.' I was wait-listed for seven classes. On one list, I was number 132. That meant I would spend the first couple weeks of the semester sitting in on three sections of the same class and begging the teachers to let me in.

They all did.

Every term since, whether registration has been simple or difficult, I've always ended up getting what I wanted—with a little patience and persistence. I have a funny feeling that's how it works for most people."

—Andy Gottesman, University of Michigan

8. IF YOU HAVE PROBLEMS, SEEK HUMAN—NOT COMPUTER— ASSISTANCE.

Many larger schools are now letting students register via the Internet or touch-tone telephone. While these methods often simplify the process, don't hesitate to call the registrar's office if you have a problem. This applies to any concerns you are having with registration. Don't wait until classes start to figure out that you are not enrolled in any.

❝ *About ten years ago, Kent State unveiled its brand-new telephone registration system. The system would supposedly eliminate all the lines, bureaucratic hassles, and confusion of the traditional registration process.*

Yeah, right!

By accident, I missed my prearranged time to call in my course selections. But I didn't worry. I had enough credit hours to be a senior, so I would just register during the time left over for seniors.

Wrong! The annoyingly sedated computer voice kept telling me that each class would put me over the number of allowable credit hours. What?

When I finally talked to someone who knew what they were doing, I found out the problem was that the computer had listed my 'hours allowable' at zero. I guess they really didn't want me to come back to school."

—Matt Kelly, Kent State University

9. DON'T WORRY ABOUT A MAJOR JUST YET.

Nobody will be asking you to declare a major as soon as you get to college. As a matter of fact, most advisors will discourage it.

You need to answer many questions before choosing a major. What kind of job are you planning on? Do you wish to attend graduate school? And of course, what interests you?

But these questions can all be answered after your freshman year, after you have decided what you like, and after you have figured out the subjects in which you excel.

And keep in mind that your major does not necessarily dictate your future career.

10. STAY CALM AND SIGN UP FOR SOME FUN COURSES.

Freshman year is a time to experiment; it's also a time to have a little fun. If you see a course that sounds interesting, try it out. You can always drop it if you don't like the first class session.

Most importantly, relax, study hard, and have fun.

CHAPTER 9

Time Management and Study Tactics

66 *How did the guy do it? He never studied. He was always asking everyone to shoot hoops, to throw the football, to crash that fraternity party, to go and hear Senator Joe Biden . . . but he got straight A's. I couldn't figure it out.*

Then it happened. I was up late doing research in the library. It was approaching midnight, but I wanted to read a few more pages on the joys of microbiology. So, I looked for the most secluded place in the library in which to stash myself and read to my heart's content. Lo and behold, there he was—Mr. Joe Cool—hitting the books like book burners were going to storm in tomorrow.

I yelled over to him, 'Caught you!' He laughed, but I knew he was a bit disappointed. That day I realized, to be successful socially and academically in college, everyone needs to learn to manage their time appropriately. Of course, not everyone has to do it the same way."

—Brandon Hsu, Stanford University

Finding Time for Everything

As you will soon find out, college offers much more than studying. In fact, finding time for everything without neglecting the books may be the most challenging test a college student faces.

Classwork: What To Expect

The days when teachers looked over your shoulder and nagged you about homework and tests are gone. In many classes, especially at larger schools, you are just a face in a crowd of 500—a "number," as the expression goes. Teachers assume you are sufficiently responsible to keep up with your work without individual attention.

The structure of most college courses reflects this philosophy. Instead of daily graded assignments and monthly tests, most college professors evaluate students solely on the basis of two or three assessments—most probably, a midterm, final, term project, or several papers. Homework, more often than not, is optional, while reading assignments are longer and less structured. For example, instead of saying, "Read these ten pages for tomorrow," the professor will remark, "Read this book before the midterm."

Just as often, the professor will not say anything about assignments but rely on the syllabus given to each student the first day of class. This item—the syllabus—is invaluable; keep it in a safe place.

With class work structured in this way, falling behind tends to haunt anyone with the slightest lazy streak. The laid-back student may find himself approaching the midterm or even the final without having read or written anything. For those who crammed in high school (and succeeded), try cramming for a final on Dostoyevsky's *The Brothers Karamozov*, Nietzsche's *Beyond Good and Evil*, Camus' *The Stranger*, Sartre's *No Exit*, and Kafka's *The Trial*— and that's just for starters. Needless to say, time management plays a large role in any successful college career.

Homework: How To Stay on Top

Self-discipline and organization are the keys to avoiding the pitfalls of procrastination. Here are a few clues to help in this war against putting things off.

1. PLOT YOUR TIME WITH A CALENDAR.

During the first week of classes, sit with a calendar and the syllabus from each class. Mark each test, paper, and assignment date, particularly noting those that fall within a day or two of each other. Such occasions are not uncommon and require extra planning.

Dr. Lauren Cohen, who has taught study strategies for twenty years at the college level, recommends plotting your course of action on a calendar. "Set daily and weekly goals on a calendar. If something comes up unexpectedly like a date, borrow time from another day, even if it means getting up an hour earlier. Marking specific deadlines on a chart and making sure to meet them enhances one's chance for success."

Expect to spend at least two nights studying for any significant exam. Papers may require more time if research is needed—sometimes you may even need to order books from another library, and that could set you back a few days. And don't make the mistake of waiting until five minutes before the paper is due to print it out. Inevitably, the printer will jam when you need it most.

Finally, don't get behind in your other classes while concentrating on one. Work ahead in the others before favoring a particular class.

 Psst . . . Many students play catch-up all year. You know the game—teacher explains one section, you read it two weeks later. Dumb! By reading the assignments before class or immediately after, the lecture material is clearer and easier to absorb.

2. ATTEND CLASS TO BOOST THE OLE G.P.A.

Much in the same regard as homework, college professors assume students are disciplined enough to attend class on a regular basis. While in smaller classes professors may be concerned with frequent student absence, few professors take role and even fewer figure attendance into the course grade. But don't let this lax attitude give you an excuse to sleep through your morning classes or bask in the sun on warm afternoons. Class attendance is critical to college success.

66 *Whatever you do, don't let those few Einsteins who can ace a test by never attending class and by sleeping on the textbook the night before trick you into using their study methods. My roommate tried to convince me that studying by osmosis was a proven method. Trust me, it isn't. In other words, just because someone can do well on a test without going to class or even looking at the book doesn't mean you can do the same."*

—Keith Vernon, University of Puget Sound

Copying notes from a more disciplined friend will not suffice. Notes should be used as an outline, reminding you of key concepts and theories covered in class. Borrowed notes will give you facts and figures but won't paint the complete picture of how the facts and figures interrelate. So, set the alarm, save the sun for the weekend, and go to class with pen and paper in hand.

If you have time, read your lecture notes at the end of each day or at least the end of the week. Students who do this find they do not have to study as much come finals week because the material already has been planted firmly in their minds.

 Psst . . . According to the Ebbinghaus Retention Curve, you lose more than 50 percent of processed information within one hour of leaving the classroom. You surrender 60 to 70 percent within 24 hours. After thirty days, 70 percent is gone.

Reviewing, rewriting, and discussing class work is the only way to effectively counteract this phenomenon. The more you engage with the material, the more you retain.

3. LEARN HOW TO STUDY EFFECTIVELY.

Face the facts! Colleges and universities are institutions of higher learning for those who want to learn. Professors expect you to study; parents expect you to study; you should expect yourself to study. Indeed, studying is a foregone conclusion. Why not make the most of it?

Okay, you're ready to hit the books for that big exam. What do you do?

First, find a suitable study environment. Some like soft music in the background. Some need people around. For most, however, a comfortable chair in a quiet room works best. Regardless, make sure you are in a place free of the temptation to socialize. Dorm rooms, particularly when shared with a roommate, seldom meet this requirement. The basement of the library or an abandoned classroom is much more accommodating.

By the way, don't fall asleep. Sleep is undoubtedly your biggest enemy. And don't study in bed; it's the kiss of death. Twenty minutes of reading in bed and, bye-bye, you've had it!

One way to avoid sleeping when you want to be studying is to use breaks as incentives. Say to yourself, "I'll go talk to some friends after I finish this chapter," or, "After I finish my chemistry, I can go out for some frozen yogurt." Don't break too often or you will frustrate your concentration and cause further distraction.

Dr. Cohen recommends working for 50 minutes and breaking for 10.

If you still have trouble getting things done or find yourself asking, "What have I been doing these last two hours?" when you were supposedly studying, make a daily schedule. Figure out what you have to do in each class, calculate how long each task will take and set up a timetable, allotting time for breaks as well.

 Psst . . . During the semester, remember to highlight important points in the chapters you read. It makes studying before an exam so much easier.

If your college offers them, lecture notes taken by other diligent students are a great way to review a course and fill in any holes in your notes. Taking old tests from the same course is also an efficient way to ensure that you are focusing on the right things. Older students may have old tests, as do many of the Greek houses. (One of the privileges of joining is that you get access to old exams.)

4. CHOOSE YOUR BATTLES WISELY.

While this book does not recommend that you skip any of your assigned homework in college, we do know from experience that everyone finds a time when there are 700 pages of Marx to read, a physics problem set to finish, and that term project for economics. Oh, and they're all due tomorrow. You will not be able to do 100 percent of the assigned work you have in college. Don't worry, no one can. If you are feeling overburdened with 500 pages of reading per week for a particular class, it's time to employ selective reading techniques. Selective reading might mean skimming until you find a part of the reading that seems significant or even asking your TA if he or she could help you figure out which areas of the syllabus deserve the most attention.

When you have three things due tomorrow and not much time left, focus on the most important one. Don't stress! It happens to everyone. And despite their reputation for being sticklers for deadlines, a lot of professors and TAs are actually very understanding and willing to grant an extension in special cases.

5. PROCRASTINATION: AVOID THE INEVITABLE.

At one time or another, every college student will get behind in his or her work—no matter how disciplined or diligent the person. A curious quirk of college life is that, come finals week, bragging rights belong to the student with the most work and the least time to complete it. Although the struggle to stay afloat in the sea of academia challenges every student, it should not be used as an excuse to drown.

66 *I had a friend who was concentrating in pre-med. He put off study-ing for his chem midterm until 10 P.M. the night before, spending his time instead at the movies and the campus hang-out. After bomb-ing the exam, he told us he did not have enough time to study. Basi-cally, he gave himself an excuse to fail."*

—Thom McDade, Pomona College

If All Else Fails . . . Pull an All-Nighter!

66 *I never pulled an all-nighter in high school. I think the latest I ever stayed up was about 3 A.M. All that changed when I went to the Uni-versity of Texas.*

Austin is a 24-hour party town. In between the 'Hook 'em Horns' football games and the jazz clubs on Sixth Street, I hardly had time to sleep, let alone work on papers all week.

So when it came time to write a big paper, I basically just planned on staying up all night. In my first semester at UT, I probably pulled . . . oh . . . about seven or eight all-nighters. Some people might say I was going overboard, but at UT that's just a way of life."

—Catherine Chen, University of Texas at Austin

Thus far, this chapter has preached the values of good time management. Indeed, nothing is more essential for continued college success. But regardless of how diligent you are, there are going to be instances when time is simply not on your side.

With so many extracurricular activities going on at college, along with classes, most students find themselves overwhelmed at certain points during the year. Fear not! For times like these, college students around the globe have invented a new concept in last-minute studying: the all-nighter.

For the most part, an all-nighter consists of staying up all night (or as late as need be) to complete a paper, finish a project, or study for a test. But willpower alone does not pull you through the wee hours. From Tulane University in New Orleans to Oxford University in England, students have turned the all-nighter into an art form. Here are five tips to help make you an artist.

Five Tips for Pulling the All-Nighter

1. GRAB SOME FOOD AND CAFFEINE, BUT KEEP IT TO A MINIMUM.

❝ *Food and stimulants are helpful to keep you going—but only in moderation. I remember once I was pulling an all-nighter to finish a research paper. Meanwhile, I had my Mr. Coffee Jr. brewing up several bucket loads of full-strength DuMond Chickory coffee. I also had a pack of fudge-covered Oreos, which I had bought in preparation for the long night.*

Three pots of coffee and a package of cookies later, I was sick to my stomach, bouncing off the walls, and staring at a vague outline. After wasting another hour or two in transit to and from the bathroom, I calmed myself down and got to work. A paper I could have finished by the early hours of the morning turned into a long and desperate project.❞

—Steve Blumenthal, Tulane University

Don't underestimate the value of coffee, a sandwich, a chocolate-chip cookie, or a pack of M&M's at 4 A.M. when the ideas aren't flowing. You may even want to plan ahead and purchase a few selected favorites from the college store before commencing with the all-nighter.

But don't drink so much caffeine or gobble down so much sugar that you're ready for outer space. Caffeine may help you to stay awake, but it can also give you the jitters. Keep it to a minimum.

2. DON'T GO NEAR YOUR BED.

❝ *It was 12:30 A.M. I was sleepy. But I couldn't hit the hay for another 5 or 6 hours because I had this organic chemistry midterm in the morning and a lot more studying to do.*

I decided to study on my bed because my desk was getting uncomfortable. Big mistake. No, HUGE mistake. The next thing I know, I look over at the clock: 9:50 A.M.! All the lights are still on, the radio is still playing, and I've got 10 minutes before a chemistry midterm, which I haven't studied for. When it came time for the final later that term, I studied at my desk—the whole time!"

—Kimara Leibowitz, Brown University

Sleep is your greatest nightmare when trying to pull an all-nighter.

Stay away from your bed, at all costs. If possible, stay away from your room. Study in your dorm's kitchen or in the library. And, if you can help it, avoid taking naps. Many a student has lain down to grab a few Z's only to wake up a few minutes before test time! So none of that "short nap" business unless a roommate is there to wake you up!

3. MAKE AN OUTLINE EARLY ON.

At 3:30 A.M., many students' minds start wandering to the sandy, spring break beaches of Mexico. So, particularly if you're going to spend the whole night writing a paper, it's a good idea to have a rough outline of the essay before you start. A general outline will give your essay some needed order. This is essential since "logical progression" is one of the first things to go when the clock strikes twelve.

 Psst . . . If you're studying for a test in the wee hours of the morning, take notes. Writing down the material on paper will help your short-term memory recall facts and figures come test time later in the day.

4. GIVE YOURSELF INCENTIVES TO CONTINUE.

❝❝ *My friends and I did some weird things to help us stay awake the night before a big paper was due. I remember once my roommate and I decided to put on our formal dresses—we're talking cinched waist, straight-skirt, fitted bodice, totally uncomfortable—and promised ourselves that we wouldn't take them off until we had finished. Needless to say, those were two papers we finished in a hurry."*

—Heather Wolfe, Amherst College

Incentives work extremely well when you've still got six pages to write and the motivation to write only two. That doesn't mean you have to put on formal attire. Other incentives, like telling yourself that a cup of coffee awaits after you finish another page, are always helpful.

5. DON'T STRESS OUT.

All-nighters are a part of college life. Enjoy them. Revel in the fact that, after four years, you probably will never pull an all-nighter again—at least not for studying purposes. The worst thing you can do is stress out. Grab some food and drink and make a night out of it. In a nutshell, see the all-nighter as an adventure, not a job.

❝❝ *My American friend, Red, defined the term 'stressing out.' Before every tutorial, he would carry on: 'Ohmigod, what am I going to do? I can't handle this. I'm going to flunk out. Help!' Finally, someone would calm him down, but he could have accomplished a lot more if he just relaxed a little. I guess that's the American spirit for you, or at least Red's."*

—Scott Parker, Oxford University

Six Quick Test-Taking Tips

College Survival has given you a few tips on how to prepare for tests. Here are a few essential suggestions on what to do while taking the actual exam.

1. LIVE FOR PARTIAL CREDIT.

Always show your work. If worse comes to worst, write *something* down, anything, even if it's your girlfriend's phone number as opposed to the correct answer. Partial credit has salvaged more than a few test scores, especially in science courses where the median score is often 40 percent or lower.

2. USE KEY WORDS AND CATCH PHRASES.

With 400 exam books to grade, a professor or teaching assistant is usually not worrying about the intricacies of your test. In fact, the grader may just have a checklist with key words and catch phrases on it. If your essay has a lot of these key words you may earn an A or B; if not, you may receive a C or D. Ugh!

3. WRITE CLEARLY.

No, this doesn't mean use good handwriting (although some professors demand it). It means write with clarity and purpose. The object is simple but contradictory: Get down as much as possible in the most logical fashion.

4. ALWAYS AGREE.

Unless you *really* know your stuff, don't disagree with the teacher. Regurgitation, however boring, is your best bet come report card time.

5. ANSWER EVERY QUESTION, IF POSSIBLE.

Don't spend 2 hours answering the first question when you have five more of equal weight staring you in the face. Bide your time and make sure to answer most completely those questions that are worth the most points.

6. DON'T STRESS OUT.

Getting uptight because you can't answer the first question is futile. Move on. If the rest of the test looks like Chinese when it's supposed to be Spanish, do the best you can. Try rewording the questions so they make more sense to you. Chances are, other students are having the same problems you are.

Excessive worrying only makes you less productive. If all else fails, refer to Tip Number 1 and pray. In short, resign yourself to the beneficence of The Curve, one of the greatest parts of a college grading system.

CHAPTER 10

Setting Goals for Success

❝ *I did a lot of goofing off in high school. While some of my friends were studying, I'd be out shooting hoops, playing cards, or the like. But all this goofing off put me in the doghouse when it came time to choose colleges.*

Most of my friends went to the University of Washington, but because of my grades, I didn't have that option. I chose the University of Portland.

From the start, I decided that I wanted to be with my friends and transfer to Washington. So, I called up the UW admissions office and asked what type of grades I needed to transfer. They told me I needed a 3.3 GPA. So, for the first semester at Portland, my book bag was my girlfriend. The library was my Friday night party palace.

When grades for first semester came out, I did a double take: 3.9! What's this? Get Harvard on the line.

It just goes to show what having a goal and following through can do. A 2.5 in high school to a 3.9 in college—even I wouldn't have put money on that one."

—Chris Scalzo, University of Portland

The Five Basic Steps of Goal Setting

Successful college students, regardless of the institution they attend, use these five steps to set goals:

1. Make a scale of priorities.
2. Set specific, measurable, and realistic long-term goals.
3. Set short-term goals.
4. Make social, personal, and academic goals.
5. Strive to meet those goals.

Goal setting does not necessarily mean sitting down with pen and paper and making a list of priorities, although often that can be extremely helpful. At the very least, however, goal setting should become a regular mental exercise.

66 *I have never actually written down a set of goals, but I still go through the process of 'goal setting' every day. I'm always asking myself, 'How am I going to get an A on this next test? What is the best way to prepare? Am I going to have to skip playing tennis tomorrow to make time for studying?'*

Goal setting, as far as I can see it, is simply a state of mind, a way of thinking about things. A goal setter makes sure he accomplishes what he needs to accomplish. He takes the necessary steps in that direction.

College is full of distractions. In fraternities, sororities, and dorms, there are always TVs blaring, people to talk to, and parties of some sort every night. It's very easy for someone who hasn't set priorities to get sidetracked."

—Greg Gottesman, Stanford University

 Psst . . . Dr. Lauren Cohen, a college professor of twenty years, recommends physically writing down long-term and short-term goals. She has done this exercise with many students and insists that it enhances one's chance for success.

1. MAKE A SCALE OF YOUR PRIORITIES.

By now, after seventeen-plus years, you have established a certain lifestyle. Perhaps you are a student, an athlete, a musician, a partier, or a combination of all of these. Without even knowing it, you have set priorities and lived by them.

College is the time to look at who you are and contrast what you see with who you want to *become*. This does not mean you shouldn't be yourself; rather, you should make room for growth and improvement.

For example, if you were a partier in high school but want to become more of a student, now is the time to change. If you were not an athlete but want to learn how to play tennis, now is the time to sign up. If you always wanted to hold a school office but never had the chance, now is the time to get involved on campus or in the community.

By making a scale of what is important to you, you will be ready to set some definite goals.

2. SET SPECIFIC, MEASURABLE, AND REALISTIC LONG-TERM GOALS.

Just saying you want to "do well" in school is not enough. Everyone wants to do well. Besides, "doing well" is not a measurable goal; what exactly is "doing well"? Is it an A or a B?

On a similar note, setting your sights on a 4.0 GPA when you never received above a 2.0 in high school is unrealistic, albeit admirable.

In the simplest of terms, set *specific*, *measurable*, and *reasonable* long-term goals. Say to yourself, "I am going to get at least a B in biology," or "I am going to get at least a 3.3 GPA" Both of these statements are specific, reasonable, and measurable.

3. SET SHORT-TERM GOALS.

Without short-term goals, long-term ones are impossible to achieve.

❝ *I had a friend who told me at the beginning of the year he would get an A in chemistry. But he ended up just being a talker For him, just having the goal was good enough."*

—Thom McDade, Pomona College

To achieve the long-term goal of an A in chemistry, this student needed short-term goals. They might have included:

1. Completing all lab assignments
2. Attending all classes
3. Finding a study partner
4. Completing course readings on time
5. Studying hard for the midterm and final

Even though you may have trouble meeting all these short-term goals, following through on most of them will help you achieve your long-term aspirations.

4. SET SOCIAL, PERSONAL, AND ACADEMIC GOALS.

Academics are only one facet of your college education. You should set social and personal goals as well as academic ones.

For most students, socializing is high on the priority list . . . only four years left before belly flopping into the real world, right?

Some of these social ambitions may include dating, getting along with your roommate, becoming more culturally aware, and learning to feel more comfortable in social situations.

Personal goals, on the other hand, may consist of balancing your checkbook each month, exercising regularly, or eating a balanced diet.

5. CONTINUALLY STRIVE TO MEET YOUR GOALS.

❝ *My friend Gary really wants to study medicine. He is a brilliant guy, and he will make a fantastic surgeon, I'm sure. However, Gary made the mistake of having a bit too much fun his first few years at Rice and pretty much blew off a lot of his schoolwork. He ended up with a 3.0 GPA at the end of his fifth semester, which is at the lower end of the spectrum for the competitive medical schools.*

Gary realized he would have to do something to redeem himself, so he spent the entire second semester of his junior year studying for the MCAT to be held that April. No more partying for Gary; he attended only two social events that semester and spent every other minute reviewing biology, chemistry, and physics. Needless to say, Gary breezed through the test.

Most of Gary's friends think he is insane for giving up four months of his life studying for a test. But Gary thinks he got a pretty good deal: studying like a madman for one term in exchange for a future."

—Rosalind Martz, Rice University

Think of how few people ever achieve their dream of becoming a Hollywood star, an Olympic champion, or the CEO of a large corporation. Obviously, no one is giving away free tickets to success. However, by prioritizing, by setting realistic long-term goals and by achieving long-term goals through short-term ones, you will be surprised at how much you can accomplish.

As Alfred Lord Tennyson once said, "'Tis better to have loved and lost than never to have loved at all." Well, you know what he meant: Go for it!

CHAPTER 11

Getting Involved

❝ *When I arrived at La Salle, I was a little afraid to devote too much time to extracurriculars. I wasn't sure how much time I would have after classes and homework and parties. What I didn't realize was how much more free time I would have in college. Granted, I had more homework than in high school, but with fewer classes in college I also had more time to get it done.*

Joining the newspaper was one of the best decisions I made. I met some of my best friends on the staff—two of my roommates and a boyfriend! It also gave me something else to do besides schoolwork. My friends who just concentrated on academics really missed out."

—Christina Roache, La Salle University

Will I Have Time to Get Involved?

Believe it or not, you're going to have a bunch of free time in college. In high school, the majority of your day was spent in the classroom. Not so in college. Most freshmen average only three hours a day in lecture; the rest of your day is yours.

Although college courses require more study time, it would be a mistake to be on a first-name basis with the local librarian. Activities outside of your course work will be just as important to your "college experience."

What Can I Get Involved In?

Most colleges offer every type of activity you have ever imagined and even some you haven't. Experiment! Try a variety of activities, some you may have done in high school and others that just sound interesting. Dan Hutter from the University of Miami said, "Don't be afraid to go a little bit wild. If

newspaper and student government don't excite you, there's a lot else out there. Skydiving . . . now that's something Mom and Dad can tell their friends about."

If you're afraid of heights, here is a list of some of the more traditional extracurriculars:

- Sports: You don't need to be a varsity athlete to exercise (See Chapter 17 about athletics and exercise for details).

- Band: If you played an instrument in high school and enjoyed it, join the band or another musical group. It's a great way to see football games for free.

- Politics: If you're a budding politician, your school's student government will have numerous elected and committee positions. Working for a cause or on a local politician's campaign are two other options.

- Journalism: If you enjoy writing, there are a lot of different student publications on campus. Some even pay you to write. Great way to make some extra money!

- Arts: Whether you are a performer or just a connoisseur, college will offer you a host of cultural opportunities in music, dance, and theater. Just because you didn't act or dance in high school doesn't mean you shouldn't try now. Many theaters offer college students the opportunity to usher and see top-rate cultural events for free.

Why Get Involved?

66 *Getting involved with College Republicans was the best decision I made in college. I came to Boston University unsure of my abilities. College Republicans gave me confidence in myself. After holding several leadership positions in the group, I was elected to the National Office of the College Republicans my senior year. The leadership skills I learned in that group will help me for the rest of my life."*

—William Spadea, Boston University

1. MAKE FRIENDS.

Usually your best friends in college will be those people who have similar interests. For that reason, extracurriculars are a great place to make lasting friendships and find future roommates.

2. RELIEVE STRESS.

Extracurriculars offer a legitimate break from the grind of schoolwork. Shooting hoops or playing in the band will let you return to Plato in a better frame of mind.

3. BUILD A RESUME.

Extracurriculars may give you some ideas about future career paths. In addition, getting involved in group activities will teach you cooperation, organization, and leadership skills. At the very least, extracurriculars are very important for an effective resume. Would you hire someone with a 4.0 grade point average and the personality of a No. 2 pencil?

4. HAVE FUN.

Let's face it, unless you're an ancient philosopher, reading books can get kind of boring. Enough said.

Will It Harm My Grades?

Contrary to what you might think, getting involved won't necessarily hurt your grades. In fact, studies have shown the opposite: people who are more involved tend to get better grades. They organize their time better and study more efficiently. As Walt Eife of Western Maryland College said, "The more things I have to do during a day, the more I get done. If I don't have anything, I just watch TV and save all my work till the last minute."

What About Community Service?

66 *At Stanford, it's very easy to get caught up in the palm trees, the academics, the people. I know a lot of students who spend four years here without ever leaving the campus. Kind of sad!*

For that reason, I have made a concerted effort to try to get out in the community and help out. I teach tennis and physical education to high school and elementary school students in East Palo Alto. It's the most rewarding thing I've done for several reasons. It keeps me in touch with the real world. It makes me feel good about myself. It also gives me the chance to make an impact on real people. You'd be surprised how much impact you can have on the life of a fifth grader."

—Greg Gottesman, Stanford University

If you're going to participate in only one extracurricular activity, consider community service. The rewards are incredible.

Most campuses have a community service center where you can get information about different projects. Some of these activities might include working on the Special Olympics, tutoring economically disadvantaged students, or building shelters for the homeless.

In the past, college students have been responsible for much positive change in our society. More than any other group, they have the free time, energy, and optimism to truly make a difference.

❝ *I remember how scared I was the first time I visited the juvenile jail. I figured I'd meet a lot of tough kids who wouldn't be interested in doing any of the activities we had planned for them.*

For the first few hours, my worst fears were confirmed. They laughed at the idea of freeze tag, rolled their eyes at making montages, and refused to do pantomimes. I was getting discouraged, to put it mildly.

Then I sat down with one of the girls and just started talking. After a while she began to open up and tell me about her past. She never knew her father, and her mom was in prison for prostitution. She herself was in jail for drug pushing, the only work she could find at age 12. When I first sat down, I thought I could teach her something about life. Little did I know I'd be the person to learn.

After that initial bonding, the girls were more excited about our games. The next few hours passed quickly and soon it was time to go. The girl I had spoken with came over and gave me the biggest hug. She told me that she had never had so much fun in her life and made me promise I'd come back. I have never felt quite like that again."

—Tara McCann, Stanford University

CHAPTER 12

Computers at College

    ❝ *Yesterday while I was over at my friend's house, I decided to check the ole e-mail. Well, I knew that something was wrong right off the bat, because every time I pressed a key on the keyboard, the computer would do something very unpredictable. I was using 'Find File' to try to locate Telnet on his computer, and I couldn't even type in Telnet without the computer just going berserk.*

Well, after some trial and error (and nagging fears that I had irretrievably damaged a very expensive piece of machinery), I determined that the key T had been reassigned to Enter, and E was now N. Fortunately (sort of), L was now E, so we had the major vowels covered. It was a triumph of human ingenuity to actually find telnet by searching for ELNE. Of course, that still didn't resolve the problem that T meant Enter. I soon gave up.

The funny thing was that we kept on forgetting about this inconvenient keyboard problem. We later tried to play computer Jeopardy. *The answer to the first question was Athens, and you can imagine the apologetic tones from Mr. Trebek as he informed each of us in turn that he was sorry, the answer was not A. Through thorough detective work (we asked his dad), we determined that a 'keyboard macro' had been set, basically customizing the keyboard for some nefarious no-goodnik. Morals of the story: never EVER set a keyboard macro; if you do, Control+Alt+Suspend Macro (or asking your dad) will save you.* ❞

—David Sivak, Harvard University

Computer Lingo

Hardware: Computer, monitor, disk drives, printer, mouse, modem, and cables; basically all the physical parts of the computer.

Software: Software, often called programs or applications, is the instructions that computer hardware needs to perform a task like word processing or playing a game.

Mouse: A traditional mouse contains a ball that rolls along the desk or mouse pad when the mouse is moved. The ball in turn spins several wheels inside the mouse, one vertically, one horizontally, and probably a third one for stability. These wheels send impulses to the computer and direct the pointer on the screen.

 Psst . . . Over time, the ball in a traditional mouse will pick up bits of dirt and lint from your desk or mouse pad and transfer them to the wheels. As dust and lint collect on the wheels, they interfere with smooth spinning. As a result, the mouse will not glide as easily and the pointer will jump from one side of the screen to the other. A simple fix is to open the bottom of the mouse, take out the ball, clean and reinsert it, and the mouse will run smoothly again.

An optical mouse replaces the ball and wheels mechanism with a small camera located on the bottom of the mouse that sees which way the surface seems to be moving and translates that information into cursor movement. Unlike a traditional mouse, which needs occasional maintenance, an optical mouse needs less frequent maintenance.

Kilobyte (K or Kb), Megabyte (meg or Mb), Gigabyte (gig or Gb): These terms refer to quantities of information. A byte is one character, a kilobyte 1,000, a megabyte 1 million, and a gigabyte 1 billion. If you must know, the next step is a terabyte, or 1 trillion.

Floppy disk: These disks come in regular and highdensity. The 3½-high-density disks (1.44 Mb) are the industry standard.

Hard drive: Non-removable magnetic disk contained within a computer used to store multiple programs and large amounts of data and text. Hard drives come in different sizes (these days, we're talking gigabytes), according to the amount of information they store.

Random Access Memory (RAM): Both RAM and hard drives are forms of memory (as are floppy disks, CD-ROMs, Zip drives, and other "drives"). But there is a big difference. RAM is more accessible memory, situated very close to the heart of the computer, the processor. In fact, RAM is the only memory that the processor can access directly. This means that in order to run a program, the processor needs to be able to hold the important parts of the program and related information in RAM. Virtual memory and other similar tricks use software to make the processor think that there is more RAM than is actually physically available by using hard-drive space and keeping only the most important information in RAM. This means that the computer probably will be able to run programs that won't fit in RAM (as long as your hard drive is not full), but they will run slower. With today's technology, 128 Mb of RAM comes standard with most new machines, but some are outfitted with as much as 256 Mb of RAM.

Megahertz (MHz): This is the unit used to measure a computer's speed. It is the number of millions of cycles per second that your processor can complete. Cycles generally correspond to operations, so the higher this number is, the better. It's not the only important number in determining a computer's speed, but it's a good reference.

Modem: A device for transmitting electronic information via telephone lines.

Bits per second (bps): The rate at which a modem can send or accept information.

Compact Disk–Read Only Memory (CD-ROM): A small plastic disk like a music CD that comes with programs, games, and/or music. CD-ROMs have much more storage space than floppy disks, but you can only save information to a CD-ROM if have a CD burner. If you choose to burn your information onto CD-ROMs, you can use CD-Rs or CD-RWs. CD-RWs allow you to reuse a disc while CD-Rs can be burned only once. CD-Rs are significantly less expensive than CD-RWs are, so most people choose to burn their information on CD-Rs.

Questions to Consider Before You Buy

1. DO I ALREADY OWN AN ADEQUATE COMPUTER SYSTEM?

The computer world changes so fast that it is hard to say what an *"adequate"* system is, because by the time this book goes to *press,* whatever was adequate today will be obsolete. So the best rule of thumb is that any computer system that is more than two or three years old is probably about to reach dinosaur status, and if you can afford it, you will want to replace such a system before heading off to school.

2. DOES THE SCHOOL PROVIDE SUFFICIENT COMPUTER FACILITIES?

Many colleges offer easily accessible computer facilities in the dormitories or libraries. For the student on a tight budget, it pays to investigate. If the computer facilities at your school are particularly good, you may not need your own computer.

Dorm-based computer centers may be ideal for the nonowner. Call the housing office once you have received your assignment and ask about computer availability. Even if you buy one, it's nice to have a backup close by.

Make sure that there are enough facilities to accommodate a good number of students. Come term-paper time, you don't want to find yourself waiting in line for a free machine.

3. WHAT TYPE OF COMPUTER DOES MOST OF THE CAMPUS USE?

Although few schools will dictate which type of computer students should use, a certain type usually emerges as the "most popular." You might want to find out ahead of time whether most students at your school use Macs (less likely) or whether they use IBM PC-compatible computers (more likely).

There are numerous benefits to owning the campus computer of choice. In case of a computer breakdown, there will be more compatible systems that are easily accessible.

4. DOES MY MAJOR REQUIRE A SPECIAL COMPUTER?

Engineering and computer science students may have special computer needs, whereas English and history majors may need to use only simple word-processing programs. Check the standards of your department before buying. A superexpensive Mac or IBM-compatible system may be overkill if all you have to do is crank out three papers a quarter and surf the Web.

Despite what you might think, you'll probably want your own computer as much for your English and history courses (to have privacy while you write) as your science courses (which may use computers for writing labs or statistical analysis). In fact, computer scientists, whose assignments require heavy programming, often find it easiest to use the computer lab's computers for several reasons. First, many computer scientists will be working there and TAs will often hold office hours there, so help is easy to find. Second, programming courses often use UNIX (an alternative to the Windows, DOS, or Macintosh operating systems), which is easiest to use in a computer lab.

Shop Smart! Six Tips on Computer Shopping

1. LOOK AT THE WARRANTY.

The most valuable part of your computer is not any of the hardware—it's the warranty. When you are shopping for a new computer, you want to make sure that your investment will last you the next four years. Make sure that the manufacturer is willing to stand by its product. Look for a warranty of at least two and preferably four years

 Psst . . . For an additional $100–$200, you can buy extra warranty protection that guarantees on-site service within 24 hours should your computer ever break down. This may be a wise investment; it means that you won't have to deal with the hassles of sending your computer back to the factory if it doesn't work, and it also means much quicker turnaround time. You should consider the warranty fees when purchasing your computer—some computers come with better warranty deals than others.

2. YOU NEED SPEED (MHz) IF YOU ARE GOING TO SURF THE WEB EXTENSIVELY OR PLAY GAMES.

Everyone talks about speed, but is it really important? New software, like the newest word processors or spreadsheets, or even the latest version of Windows, can seem slow because they expect people to have new computers. But, in fact, if you use older software for things like word processing, you'll probably get the same results, and your computer will never seem slow.

The biggest need for speed comes from the Internet. The speed of your computer will affect the speed at which you can download information (software, pictures, sounds, movies) from the Internet. Also, since high-quality sounds and pictures and movies are now more readily accessible, you may want a computer that can view pictures, play sounds, and watch videos, without too much delay.

Finally, faster computers mean bigger and badder games. The latest games, which will be readily available from friends or the Internet, make impressive hardware demands. The newest version of Quake will make even the fastest machines jerk.

So there are many uses for speed, but it is probably not imperative that you have the fastest computer around. If you're only going to use your computer for word processing or spreadsheet work, you'll never notice the difference between a 600 MHz and a 900 MHz machine. If you want to play games and surf the Web, and you don't want to borrow a friend's computer or walk to the lab, then you'll want to look into the latest and fastest hardware.

3. MAKE SURE YOUR COMPUTER COMES WITH THE RIGHT COMPONENTS.

If you know what programs you want to run, make sure that your new computer's hardware components will be powerful enough to operate that software.

Furthermore, if you know that you will be dialing in to your school's network, then you will want to make sure that you have a pre-installed modem, whereas if you will be using an Ethernet jack to log on, you might want a machine that comes with an Ethernet card. (For more on these types of components, see Chapter 13, The Internet.)

4. BE CAREFUL IF YOU BUY A USED COMPUTER.

66 *Before leaving for college, I went shopping for a new computer. I couldn't decide between laptop and desktop because although I wanted a laptop, I could really only afford a desktop, so I decided to check out the classified ads for a used laptop. I found a laptop in the paper for about half the price of a new one, and I thought to myself, 'Great! It's only a year and a half old!' I bought the machine and was so pleased at my good fortune . . . for a little while. One by one, things started to go wrong. The screen would freeze up. The mouse stopped working. Memory started to malfunction. Finally, I was working one day and the screen just went dark. Bye-bye. In a matter of months, my very cheap computer had become a* *very expensive doorstop. I got my next machine new, and it came with a full four-year warranty, so I don't have to deal with the unexpected."*

—Daniel Baer, Harvard University

Used systems of *recognized* brand names (such as IBM, Compaq, Dell, or Apple) may be good buys, but beware! Technology changes so quickly and the computer market is so competitive that newer and faster systems with warranties and even free servicing are not much more expensive than used ones.

Don't ask a used-computer seller what the system originally cost. That doesn't matter—you need to find out how much the system is worth today! A two-year-old system that works fine and cost $3,000 when it was new might be a bad buy compared to a *new* computer that's twice as fast and half as expensive. Price out new computers before you buy an old one.

For a nominal fee, used computers can be checked out for internal damage by a local computer repair facility. Obscure brands may not be repairable and are not worth the risk.

5. PORTABLE COMPUTERS ARE GREAT FOR SCHOOL BUT PRICEY.

Portable (or laptop) computers have a lot of advantages—and disadvantages. New ones are just as powerful as the computers that sit on your desk, yet they are small enough to fit into your backpack. Portability is a huge plus. You can bring a laptop computer with you to the library to write a paper or into the classroom to take notes. Because of their portability, laptops often must be well suited for networks and have more video hardware than a corresponding desktop. In fact, they are often better suited for watching streaming video over the Internet.

The major disadvantage of a laptop computer is price. Expect to pay about 50 percent more for portability. In addition, the screen, keyboard, and mouse on portable computers are smaller and less user-friendly than on larger desktop computers. Moreover, because laptops are small enough to pick up, they also get dropped every so often, which may lead your computer to become angry and perhaps not turn on the next time you hit the power switch. Another major problem is theft. If you can transport your computer comfortably in your backpack, so can someone else. If you buy a portable computer, be careful not to leave your computer alone in public.

6. CHECK OUT YOUR SCHOOL'S TECHNOLOGY CENTER/ BOOKSTORE AND THE INTERNET FOR GOOD DEALS ON NEW COMPUTERS.

Many college bookstores and technology centers offer special student discounts on computers and printers. Check out these prices before buying from other computer stores or looking in the newspaper or on the Internet. One of the advantages of buying on campus is that computer repair is usually easily accessible, and sometimes you can get free service at the school's center if you buy your computer from them.

Mail-order purchases may save you a few bucks and sales tax, but be sure to investigate the company before buying over the phone. The best Internet/ mail-order firms, such as Gateway and Dell, usually offer good prices, at-home service and phone support.

And, of course, there is always the Internet. If you know the specific model, or if you can list a set of specifications for the machine you want (for instance, an Intel Pentium 4 processor at 1.8 GHz, with 512 Mb SDRAM memory at 133 MHz, etc.), then you might check out several Internet sites, such as http:// www.dell.com, to see what kind of price you can get through the Web.

Use and Abuse of Computers

1. BE SURE TO SET YOUR COMPUTER TO AUTOMATICALLY SAVE YOUR WORK EVERY 10 MINUTES.

These days all word processing programs have a setting that allows you to program your machine to save your work automatically every few minutes. Definitely make sure that you have the AutoSave function set!

If your computer does crash (or rather, *when* your computer does crash), don't panic! Your machine will probably recover your file when you reboot. If it doesn't immediately surface when you turn the machine back on, find a friend who knows how to access your "temp" files; it might be in there. You can also use the "find file" command and then limit the search to files that were recently updated—there won't be many that were modified in the last five minutes. Get help if you need it, because chances are that your material is not lost, or at least, not all lost.

2. KEEP YOUR COMPUTER IN A COOL PLACE AND AWAY FROM FOOD.

Computers located too close to a vent or radiator may decide to take the day off due to heat exhaustion. Soda pop, milk, and beer also have contributed to many a system's downfall. Magnets are a bad idea, too. Keep them far away from your computer and floppy disks.

3. WHEN BORROWING, ALLOW YOURSELF PLENTY OF TIME.

Woe to the student who needs to borrow a friend's computer only to be told that the friend has 700 resumes to print out before morning.

Establish a borrowing policy early in the year. The owner has the final word.

4. GET TO KNOW A COMPUTER GURU.

You know who they are. Those students who never lose papers, whose megacomputers seem to take up an entire room. There is no magic involved—these folks really know what they're doing, and they're usually glad to help you out of a computer bind.

Your school might have a team of user assistants who will come to your room if and when you have computer problems. If so, get that number and keep it handy for times of crisis!

5. THINK ABOUT ADDING YOUR COMPUTER TO A FAMILY INSURANCE POLICY.

66 *It was one week before my freshman year began, and I was so excited. My new IBM laptop had arrived a few days earlier and I was exploring the games and programs on my new computer. Nothing can describe the look of horror on my mother's face when I grabbed the machine with damp hands and it went flying to the kitchen floor. The monitor was cracked in half—I hadn't even had it a week!*

Luckily, my dad had added the computer to our insurance policy when it arrived, so the insurance company picked up the tab for the necessary repairs—about $1,000 worth!"

—Sarah Brierley, Harvard University

As an added precaution against breakdowns, you might want to have someone check up on your computer every year or so. Most computer service stores will do a diagnostic check for $30–$40. It might save some hassles later.

 Psst . . . If you own a laptop, you can purchase a lock that attaches your computer to your school desk with a heavy duty cable. Laptops are normally easy prey for thieves, but this small investment can change that.

6. PROTECT AGAINST VIRUSES.

Most schools have some viruses running around, and not just in the sick bay. Be careful when you borrow floppy disks (to use with your computer) or download material via the Web. You should make sure that your computer is equipped with good virus protection software before heading off to school. The newer the software, the more viruses it will be able to recognize.

7. DON'T LET THE COMPUTER BECOME AN ENEMY.

Don't let that little glowing screen become an adversary. If you plan correctly and take all the necessary precautions, the computer will be your most useful tool at college—next to your brain. By the way, the most common problem new students have with their computers at school—forgetting to plug them in!

CHAPTER 13

The Internet

" *Before coming to college, I had hardly ever used the Internet, even for e-mail. The only thing I used a computer for in high school was to write essays, and that was under protest. Even when I heard stories about the wonders of the Internet, I didn't believe them; I thought it was just something for those techno-freaks who live in the computer lab.*

Wow, was I in for a surprise! I don't know how I ever lived with out e-mail! I probably exchange 25–30 e-mails a day with everyone from friends, to professors, teaching assistants, members of clubs that I am in, etc.

And I use the Web for everything . . . buying plane tickets, finding books, doing research, finding friends from high school, getting a statistic for a paper, even picking up the broadcast of the Denver Broncos Football Network from the local radio station back home.

I know that people survived for centuries in colleges without e-mail and access to the Web, but I can't imagine how they did."

—Daniel Baer, Harvard University

The Internet—It's Not a Choice Anymore

You may have dabbled a bit with the Internet before coming to college. Hey, you may have even dabbled a lot, but chances are that while you were in high school you used the Internet mainly for entertainment value . . . and why not?

No matter how much you know about the Internet already, in college the Internet is going to play a much more important role in your life. At many schools, professors post assignments and class announcements on the Web. And e-mail has become the preferred method for contacting a professor to beg for an extension on that last term paper.

This chapter is designed to give you the lowdown (and much more!) on how you can be the Internet-savvy student that you always dreamed you might become. Okay, maybe you didn't exactly dream about it, but at least this chapter will give you the facts you need for the ever-increasing role that the Internet will play in your college experience. We'll start off with the technical side of things, because in order to understand the Internet's capabilities, it is helpful to understand how it functions in the first place.

Internet Basics

What is the Internet anyway? BRACE YOURSELF—here comes the full explanation!

The latest computer revolution is the computer "network." If computers can talk to each other, they take on a whole new role. No longer are they just complicated adding machines; now they can allow people to communicate and interact in a new way. A network is any group of computers that can communicate with each other. The largest network is the Internet.

If you connect two computers with a wire, there are many ways that they can communicate, depending on how the computer is programmed to interpret the signals it receives from the wire. Each of these different ways of interpreting signals is a protocol at the network layer. The Internet uses the *Internet Protocol* (IP).

For computers to communicate, they need names for each other. Computers on the Internet refer to each other in terms of IP addresses, which are unique to each computer. Each address is a set of four numbers between 0–255, separated by *dots*, or periods. For example, 192.45.235.3 or 10.219.114.11 are both valid IP addresses. Computers use a hierarchical approach to finding other computers. If only two computers are on a network, it's easy for one computer to send a message, since there's only one possible way to send it. But for a network like the Internet, a wide area network or WAN, the network must be divided into smaller networks, or *subnets*. If one of the computers of the smaller network is connected to the Internet, then the entire network can be connected to the Internet. All of the computers on a network will have the first few numbers of their IP address in common. So you might expect the computers with IP addresses 192.80.0.4 and 192.80.0.5 to be on the same subnet.

Although numbers are ideal for computers, people need to translate IP addresses into words. However, in an attempt to capture the spirit of the IP address, computer names are still composed of several words separated by dots. For example, you might recognize one of the following: fas.harvard.edu or stwing.upenn.edu or athena.mit.edu or whitehouse.gov. Computers that are connected to the Internet use DNS (domain name server) to translate between names and IP addresses (numbers), so you don't have to know the numbers in an IP address, only the name. The first thing a computer does with a name is translate it to an IP address that it can understand. Without that crucial step, networking is impossible.

There are several major suffixes for computer names: .com (for businesses), .edu (for education), .org (for organizations), .gov (for government), .mil (for the military), and country suffixes (.au for Australia, .jp for Japan, .fr for France, .ca for Canada, and so on). Each network usually ends with the same two words, such as harvard.edu, mit.edu, dell.com, microsoft.com, or whitehouse.gov. IP addresses and names are chosen locally by the network administrator and on a large scale by a central organization that is licensed by the government.

What Are All These Acronyms and Techno Terms?

One of the most unfortunate aspects of new technology is that every innovation in the technological world seems to be accompanied by an innovation in the vocabulary world. The Internet is no exception . . . and although you may have heard a lot of these terms before, it might be helpful to take a quick glance at the techno mumbo-jumbo before moving on.

Browser: Web browsers like Netscape Navigator and Microsoft Internet Explorer send a simple message: a request for a particular page to a waiting Web server. The server's only job is to process the request, retrieve the page, and send it to the browser.

HTTP: HTTP stands for Hypertext Transfer Protocol. Remember that a protocol is simply a set of rules that people agree upon as a convention. Network protocols are the rules for a language, like a grammar, and application protocols are rules for a program, like the rules of a game. HTTP is the protocol of the World Wide Web.

HTML: HTML stands for Hypertext Markup Language, the coding language in which Web pages are written. HTML contains text, formatting, and graphics information that can be read by any browser, regardless of the computer system it's running on.

ISP: ISP stands for Internet Service Provider, which is the name used for companies who sell access to the Internet. AOL and Earthlink are two of the largest ISPs.

LAN: LAN stands for Local Area Network, a small network of computers connected by the same physical wire. Your school LAN will most likely use Ethernet cables (which plug into the wall in jacks that look like oversized phone jacks). Most LANs are restricted (by the speed of light) to a definite length, about 500 meters, in order to be effective. So LANs are necessarily small. Several LANs can be connected together in a larger network. The network of a university or a moderate to large company is often composed of 10 to 200 LANs.

Ethernet Card: The hardware required for a computer to be able to be part of a LAN.

Links: What is the secret to the Web's popularity? The thing that makes HTML special is the links. Links are simply words or pictures on one page that a person can click to get to another page. Clicking on a link is no different from simply typing the address of the new page into your browser. Links give the impression that there is some sort of connection between the two pages, but from the computer's point of view, it is simply requesting one page, then requesting another page.

Modem: This is the computer hardware device that allows your computer to transmit and receive data over telephone lines. It is basically a phone within your computer.

Search Engine: Search engines are your tool for exploring the Internet and finding what you need. Yahoo!, Excite, and Google all have popular search engines.

Server: A server is a computer that acts as the interface between computers on the network. When you see an e-mail address like picasso@rcomail.com, the "rcomail" identifies the server where that person's account is held. You can think of servers as post offices. A zip code identifies the post office where a letter will be sent, and then the employees of that post office deliver the letter to personal mailboxes. With e-mail, messages are sent to the server identified in the e-mail address, and then the server files them into the appropriate mailbox, or account. Servers also store the data for Web pages on the World Wide Web. When you type a Web-site address like www.beachcollege.edu, the address identifies the server that stores the data for the Web site that you want to see.

T1/T3 Line: T1 and T3 lines are special kinds of cable used in LANs. They are capable of carrying more information at higher speeds than a normal phone line. T3 lines are faster than T1 lines.

Telnet: Telnet sites are located on the Internet and allow users from all over the world to access a computer system, such as a library card catalog.

URL: URL stands for Uniform Resource Locator, which is the full address of a Web page; for example, http://www.whitehouse.gov is a URL.

WWW: WWW is the abbreviation for the World Wide Web, which is the global network of all computers that are connected via the Internet. But WWW refers specifically to the HTTP material on the Internet (Web pages), not to e-mail.

How To Get Internet Access

Before you can withdraw cash from an ATM, you gotta have the card, before you can take mom's car out for a spin you gotta get the keys out of her purse, and before you can fire off an e-mail to your best friend, you gotta get access to the Internet.

SCHOOL NETWORKS (LANS)

These days, many schools are installing network connections in all dorm rooms, so if you are living on campus, there is a good chance that your room will be set up with Internet access when you arrive. If this is the case, you will need to get an *Ethernet card* for your PC if you want to have access to the Internet from your room. If your computer was purchased recently, it may have come with an Ethernet card already installed, so you will want to figure out if you have an Ethernet card hidden somewhere in your computer or if you will need to purchase one. A good way to determine whether you have an Ethernet card is to check the back of your PC for a jack like the one described above.

Ethernet cards are not cheap . . . they can cost up to $200, depending on what kind of computer you have. However, if you can scrounge together the dough, you will definitely appreciate the added convenience of having the Internet in your room.

Most schools that have a school-wide network will offer Ethernet cards for sale when you arrive on campus. You will want to skim through the volumes of forms and information sheets that your school sends you over the summer to see if you can buy Ethernet cards directly from your school. If you can, it's probably best to just wait until you get there to buy it; that way you know that you have exactly the card you need for the school's network, and if it doesn't work, you will be able to exchange it easily.

Your Ethernet card should come with a cord that looks like an oversized phone cord, which plugs into the jack in the wall in your room on one end and into your Ethernet card on the other end—if you have a desktop computer. If you have a laptop, this cord plugs into a connector, which is called a dongle (yes, this is actually the technical, industry standard name for this piece of equipment —dongle, hmm). Anyway, the dongle gets plugged into the Ethernet card, and presto . . . you are ready to surf the Web.

You will have to open your e-mail account and register your jack before you have full access to the Internet. (You should receive information and instructions from your school about setting up your account.)

MODEMS AND ISPS

These days, almost any new computer comes with a modem already installed. If your school does not have a LAN set up, or if you are living off campus, then you will need to use a modem for Internet access. A modem will give you access to the Internet through the phone line, whereas a network connection using an Ethernet card uses lines that are designed expressly for computer networking.

You can get Internet access using a modem in one of two ways. First, you can "dial in" to your school's campus computer system. To do this, ask for information and instruction from your school. Assuming that your school has a system into which you can dial, this is probably the best option because it is

FREE! The second option is opening an account with an ISP, such as AOL, or the various local ISPs. Most of these companies charge a monthly fee for Internet access of around $20 to $30.

If you are living offcampus, then you should try to consult with your future roommates to make sure that at least one of you has the equipment and setup for Internet access. Make sure that you check with your school to see if it can help you get free access to the Internet from your off-campus housing before you spend money subscribing to one of the for-profit ISPs.

E-Mail—The Ins and Outs

If you are planning to spend hours on the phone with your friends from high school, forget it, especially if they are out of town. Long-distance phone bills add up pretty quickly. In college, you will probably use e-mail more than any other means of communication. It doesn't take long to discover that e-mail is the best way to communicate with professors/TAs, other students, friends, members of a club that you are in—whoever. But before you get hooked on e-mail, here are a few quick hints.

1. YOU CAN SEND THE SAME E-MAIL TO MORE THAN ONE PERSON AT THE SAME TIME.

To send the same message to multiple parties, simply address the e-mail to one person and then type all other addresses that you want the message sent to right next to the first address (usually you have to separate them by a comma or semicolon) or in the "cc:" (carbon copy) field. Note that you can also put a message in the "bcc:" (blind carbon copy) field, which allows you to send a message to another party without letting anyone else but you and the recipient know that you sent the message. For example, if you are trying to convince a friend via e-mail that he should date your roommate, you might send a "bcc:" copy to your roommate so that she is aware of your best efforts.

2. YOUR E-MAIL PROGRAM HAS AN ADDRESS BOOK WHERE YOU CAN STORE E-MAIL ADDRESSES FOR FUTURE REFERENCE.

You can also set your e-mail program to recognize nicknames. So instead of typing out MarionSmith@aol.com every time, you can just type Mom and the program will send it to your mom's e-mail address.

3. PLEASE DON'T SEND CHAIN E-MAILS!

You may get tons of e-mails saying things like "send this e-mail to 230 of your closest friends before tomorrow or you will be run over by a 1967 Russian tank on your way to breakfast." People who start these e-mails are evil and in violation of Web etiquette. All they do is fill up the e-mail inboxes, and they are a big nuisance. If someone sends you a chain e-mail, just hit the Delete button.

4. BE CAREFUL WITH YOUR REPLY COMMAND.

Make sure that when you are replying to an e-mail that was sent to a list of people you don't reply to everyone on that list. Most programs have a "Reply" command as well as a "Reply to All." There is a difference!

If you find yourself receiving lots of e-mail from an organization or company and you want to get off their list, then reply to one of the e-mails and write the following message in the Re: line: UNSUBSCRIBE.

5. DON'T GET ADDICTED!

You may scoff if you don't use e-mail much right now, but e-mail can get addictive. Seriously, you'll be sitting at your desk, trying to get through your sociology paper and the e-mail program will start to sing, and like a siren's call, it will seduce you to procrastinate for hours. Don't let yourself waste time by checking e-mail 1,000 times a day.

6. DON'T USE INAPPROPRIATE LANGUAGE OR SEND INAPPROPRIATE MATERIALS OVER THE WEB.

Some schools make you sign or agree to a contract that says you will not use inappropriate language on the Internet. You also may be discouraged or prohibited from sending pornographic materials via the Web. Sometimes a joke can be misinterpreted, and you will find yourself trying to explain your sense of humor to older administrators whose mission it is to make an example out of you. And never forget, those "private" e-mail messages you send are anything but private. Your message is stored on your computer, the recipient's computer, and on the server it passes through. If the recipient decides to forward it on to someone else, well . . . you get the picture.

7. WATCH OUT FOR VIRUSES.

The nastiest computer viruses are now sent via e-mail attachments. They have innocuous-sounding names like "Love Bug" and "Melissa," and catchy sayings in the Re: line like "Check this out." Viruses can break into your friends' e-mail Contacts folders, so infected e-mails often come from your best buddies without them knowing it. The best way to avoid viruses is to not open e-mail attachments unless you know exactly what those attachments are. In general, attachments whose file extensions end in .doc, .xls, .ppt are safe to open. Attachments whose file extensions end in .vbs are generally dangerous. If you are uncertain, even a little bit uncertain, just say no. Also, make sure that your computer is equipped with virus-protection software and that the virus protections are updated with the latest virus information.

Grab Your Computer . . . Let's Go Surfin'

The World Wide Web is a terrific resource for today's college student. The following section lists ways to get the most out of the Internet. Of course, the possibilities are endless, but hopefully the ideas below will get your brain crankin'.

1. EXPLORE CAMPUS.

If you have Internet access at home, you can check out your school's Web site over the summer. Depending on the size of your school, it might have a whole host of different resources available on the Web, anything from pictures of the dorms, to a course catalog, to the latest edition of the school newspaper. Check out your e-campus, and get to know the resources that your school makes available on the Web.

2. FIND OUT ABOUT YOUR NEW TOWN.

The Web is a great way to find out about the town where your school is located. If your school is in a small town, then you may be limited in the type of information you can find. If your school is in a city, then you should be able to check up on all the best nightspots, movie theaters, museums, sports events, and more just by clicking your mouse.

3. CHAT WITH FRIENDS.

With today's chat programs you can talk to your friends online just like you talk on the phone, except you type what you say. Chat programs are available most anywhere, and of course there are online chat rooms too. But if you like to visit chat rooms, be careful. Don't give out your address or too many personal details to someone online.

66 *My roommate freshman year was always on the Net in chat rooms and stuff. Seriously, she would stay up to all hours of the night 'chatting' with everyone else who was crazy enough to be up at that hour. And that was all good, until one day I came home from class and the phone rang. 'Hi, this is Chad, calling from Atlanta,' then there was Brian from Albany, Kyle from Idaho—all these people who had met my roommate online and now wanted to talk on the phone. Some of them even wanted to come to school and meet her in person. Our phone kept ringing with my roommate's cyberpals, and not only did it get annoying, but it was a bit eerie having all these strangers call up."*

—Monica Pearo, CU Boulder

Instant messaging (IM) is the latest fad. It lets you communicate with other friends online in much the same way that e-mail does. However, instant messaging allows you to communicate in real time. Many ISPs now have instant messaging programs, so you are likely familiar with the concept. If you have never tried it before, you'll find that IM is like e-mail on steroids. Some of the same rules already mentioned for e-mail apply for instant messaging.

4. FIND YOUR WAY AROUND.

The first few days in a new city can be disorientating to say the least. Many cities have an online resource that allows you to type in your location and where you want to go and then—presto—it produces a personalized map showing you how to get from point A to point B. Yahoo! (www.yahoo.com) has a similar service under its "Maps" section, as do www.mapquest.com, www.expedia.com, www.msn.com, and other sites.

5. SHOP FOR COMPUTERS.

If you're in the market for computers or computer equipment, the Web is a great place to look. Even if you don't buy a machine on the Web, you will have access to hundreds of dealers, and you are sure to discover the best price for any particular component you might want. Shopper.com is a great site for comparing prices on computers and other items you might want to buy online or offline.

6. LOOK FOR SOFTWARE.

Before you go buy new software, make sure that it is not available on the Web. Go to the software producer's Web site to check out the latest products and look for free stuff. Even if you can't get the programs you need for free, you may be able to sample some programs before buying so that you can make a more educated purchase.

And before you buy any special software for course work, make sure that your school doesn't offer it for free on the school network.

❝ *Once my roommate came home with mountains and mountains of computer software. He hadn't on a whim gone out and bought lots of cool games but had gone out on a whim and bought virtually every nongame piece of software on the market. He had the latest versions of the best mathematical packages, the most feature-filled word processors, spreadsheets, databases, etc. He had so much Adobe software we suspected he was sleeping with a salesperson. At some point (when he was gone) the three of us estimated that he had spent probably about $5,000 on software, all in a single fateful afternoon. The ironic twist is that except for Mathematica, I don't think he opened, let alone used, a single one of those packages. They just sat triumphantly on his bookcase, taking up the space he would need for his school stuff and his math book library (see Tip 7). Actually, no, the true ironic twist is that while he spent all this money, I was getting virtually all the same stuff for free off the Harvard general software archives, which are open to all members of the Harvard community."*

—David Sivak, Harvard University

Psst . . . There is a lot of great software available on the Net, but computer viruses can be transmitted when you download files. So be careful, download from reliable sites, and when in doubt, save the file to a disk rather than downloading directly to your hard drive.

7. SHOP FOR BOOKS.

Campus bookstores are notoriously expensive, so when you get your reading list you might want to check to see if any of the online booksellers have the titles you need. Online bookstores often offer discounts, and some smaller online bookstores are specifically geared toward students. Check out www.amazon.com and www.bn.com, which are two of the largest online book sellers.

8. SHOP FOR CDS.

If your college is not located near a music store that suits your taste, never fear! It's so easy to get a CD online. Some online music stores even have samples that allow you to hear part of a CD before you buy. Check out www.amazon.com and www.cdnow.com.

9. FIND TRAVEL INFORMATION.

Online travel agencies are a big plus for college students. Student-geared sites such as www.statravel.com and more mainstream sites like www. travelocity.com, www.orbitz.com, and www.expedia.com all offer a variety of services. You can check flight availability and price information on many different airlines all at once, and you can even book your tickets online. As an added bonus, most of these sites offer a service of e-mailing you when special fares go into effect for specified areas. So you will always know when you can get those tickets home for spring break for $139 instead of $289. Amtrak and Greyhound also have great Web sites that make trip planning much easier.

10. SURF THE LIBRARY.

Of course, the Web is also useful for academic purposes. Chances are that your school's library has a Telnet site that will allow you to search the card catalog from the comfort of your own room. No more sitting in uncomfortable wooden chairs in front of beat-up computer terminals searching for those little pencils that are about an inch long to write down card catalog numbers! You can do all your research from your room and then just drop by the library to pick up the books you want. (If you need help accessing Telnet software, ask a lab/ user assistant at your school. Also, you may be able to access your school's and other schools' library Telnet systems directly from your school's Web site.)

11. FIND STATISTICS.

If you are looking to impress a professor with the latest statistics on a particular subject, there is no better place to find those figures than the Web. Statistical and census bureaus for many countries keep their information online and available. You can find out the level of unemployment for Finland during the last two months in a matter of minutes. Google.com, a popular search engine, is a great place to begin your search.

12. GO JOB HUNTING.

Internet job listings are a great resource. Your school might have a Web site with student job listings and, if not, the local newspaper probably will. Plus, if you know a particular company that you would like to work for, say as a summer job, then you can go to that company's Web site and there will likely be a page about "Human Resources" or "Job Opportunities." If you are looking for general job listings, check out www.monster.com or www.hotjobs.com.

13. READ A LOCAL OR NOT-SO-LOCAL NEWSPAPER.

All major metropolitan US papers have an online edition, so if you're in LA and want to read about what is going on at home in Boston, just go to the *Boston Globe*'s Web site. Furthermore, if you want the latest sports scores (check out www.espn.com) or if you are a finance buff, hook into specialty sites geared to sports and business. News Web sites, such as www.cnn.com or www. abcnews.com, make it easy to keep tabs on what's happening back home. Sometimes you can even tap into the local radio station's broadcast, although you may have to purchase the broadcasting feature.

14. FIND FRIENDS.

❝ *My boyfriend took off to North Carolina for a while one time, and when he got back, he kept getting phone messages from this girl named Estelle. So I decided to do some detective work on the Web. I searched Estelle's college's home page, found the section of student home pages, and quickly found the right one. Okay, so this story makes me sound like a psycho-jealous girlfriend, but in the process, I found out how easy it is to find old friends . . . or enemies on the Web!"*

—Joan Schunck, CU Boulder

Whether it is someone you haven't seen in a few months or in a few years, the various electronic white pages and people finders that are available on the Web may soon make paper phone books all but obsolete. If you need to find someone in the next state or in another country, chances are you can find them online, especially if they are Internet users themselves. Check out Yahoo!'s "People Search" or www.whowhere.lycos.com. To find old high school friends, www.classmates.com is a terrific resource for current contact information.

15. GET HELP WITH YOUR FINANCES.

Many banks allow you to review account information and even pay your bills online. Check with your bank to find out what services they offer from their Web site or perhaps using a special software package.

Plus, surf the web for information on scholarships, fellowships, and other available financial aid programs. There are several online databases that can help you locate tons of cash that is available to help with those hefty tuition bills.

16. PLAY GAMES.

The Internet now is a great place to play games (even interactive ones), and depending on the speed of your computer, the user experience can be as good as a CD-ROM or gaming console. Most of the portal sites like Yahoo! and MSN have game sites. For 3D games, check out www.wildtangent.com. Be careful, though. Games, like e-mail, can be very addictive.

17. FIND GREAT DEALS AND UNUSUAL STUFF.

Ebay is a great place to find almost anything you can imagine, from Batman Pez dispensers to old CDs to used automobiles. The auction format also enables you to get some good bargains. And it's fun to look at what people are selling. Amazon.com has almost anything you might want, with great service. For closeout bargains and deeply discounted prices, check out www.overstock.com where you can find everything from sporting goods to computers to luggage. Shopper.com, as mentioned earlier, is a good place to do comparison shopping—something the Internet makes a whole lot easier. To buy at most Web sites, you will want to have a credit card and good control over your spending. Chapter 23 on Banking at College discusses these issues in more depth.

18. JUST EXPLORE.

The preceding tips are just a few of the many ways that you can use the Internet in college. You will find many more. Take an hour some evening and just surf around. Put the Internet to work for you. Have fun!

Setting Up Your Own Web Page

Many schools offer students a bit of space on the school's server to develop and maintain a personal Web page. To find out if your school offers this service, just ask the school's computer user assistance office. Alternatively, there are several companies on the Internet that will host your Web page either for free or for a nominal fee.

Of course, you will probably want to learn HTML (or become close friends with someone who knows HTML). If you want to design your own Web page, HTML is pretty easy to teach yourself. There are online tutorials available, and, of course, there are books in your local bookstore that will help you get the hang of it.

Also, many programs (such as Microsoft Word and PowerPoint) have an option to save text as HTML.

If you do decide to create your own Web page, you can put your resume online for potential employers to look at, as well as any other information that you might want to share with friends and guests.

Welcome To the World of Cyberstudents

Whatever happens, the Internet will inevitably play a major role in your college experience. Take advantage of the resources available, but don't end up lost in space . . . or rather, in cyberspace.

CHAPTER 14

The Minority Experience

66 *I was a little bit apprehensive about my first Indian Students Association meeting. As a freshman, I didn't know any of the other students, and I didn't know what to expect. But once the meeting started, I realized it really wasn't bad. Since my first meeting, I've developed some of my closest friendships with other members that are based on our common experiences as South Asians in America.*

If you're a minority student, I definitely would recommend going to some of the functions. It makes the university a little less intimidating."

—Anitha Venugopal, Cornell University

No "Single" Minority Experience

Writing a chapter about the minority experience is difficult because there is no "single" minority experience in college (or anywhere else for that matter). The goal of this chapter, then, is not to define the minority experience, but to provide a list of issues for minority students to think about and perhaps to offer a few words of wisdom from those who have been there before. In this chapter, the term "minority" is used broadly to encompass women, students of color, students of different religions, and students who are gay, lesbian, or bisexual.

Minority Group Activities

66 *During my first and second years, I just went to meetings and helped arrange things. But my junior and senior years I coordinated Womenspeak (a monthlong cultural celebration of women) and Students for Reproductive Freedom (a pro-choice group). One of the* *things that I liked about being involved in women's activities was that it was a great way to establish relationships with older students who became mentors. The Women's Center also became a safe place in what sometimes felt like a male-dominated community."*

—Elizabeth Nevins, Amherst College

Most normal-sized colleges have activities and groups run by and for minority students. If you are a minority student, you probably will find yourself wondering early on if and how much you should become involved in minority student activities. The answer is different for each individual. Here are some key questions to consider:

1. HOW IMPORTANT IS IT FOR YOU TO FEEL PART OF A LARGER GROUP?

The first year of college can be a difficult time of adjustment. Minority students, perhaps even more than other students, may feel alone or isolated, both in the classroom and in the residence halls. Affiliation with a minority group may provide you with a sense of belonging and make adjusting to the first year easier.

2. HOW MUCH TIME ARE YOU WILLING AND ABLE TO DEDICATE TO MINORITY ACTIVITIES?

Chances are, you will want to participate in numerous activities on campus, both minority and nonminority related. Belonging to several campus groups can be very time-consuming—group meetings are notoriously long. You need to consider time constraints when planning your level of commitment. Don't overburden yourself! One student's advice: "Don't be afraid to say 'no' if you don't have time to help organize an event or attend a meeting."

3. WHAT ARE THE POSSIBLE SOCIAL/POLITICAL IMPLICATIONS OF INVOLVEMENT AND HOW WILL YOU DEAL WITH THEM?

You should realize that group involvement may put you in some uncomfortable situations. For example, female students who become heavily involved with the women's center on campus often are surprised to find out that they are now labeled "radical feminists" merely because of this association. While labeling of this sort should not discourage your involvement, it is something to think about before becoming involved. If you choose to respond to other students who question your reasons for affiliation, honesty is usually your best weapon. Tell them exactly why it is important for you to be involved. Usually other students respond well to sincerity and honesty.

List of Minority Groups/Activities

Students of Color:

- Student associations (such as Black Students Association)
- Cultural centers
- Minority fraternities and sororities
- Community service projects that serve the local minority community
- Theme houses/residences
- Musical, theatrical, and dance groups related to cultural heritage
- Discussion groups covering minority issues

Women:

- Women's Student Association
- Women's Center
- Community service projects for women, such as battered women's shelters, and rape crisis hotlines.
- Sororities and other all-female social groups
- Musical, theatrical, and dance groups related to women's issues
- Discussion groups covering women's issues
- Women's political action groups

Gay, Lesbian, and Bisexual:

- Student center for gay, lesbian, and bisexual students
- Sexuality discussion groups

- Political action groups
- Social activities for members of the community
- Events celebrating alternative lifestyles

Students of Different Religions:

- Religion-based student associations
- Fraternities or sororities
- Discussion groups covering religious issues
- Political action groups
- Theme houses/residences
- Eating clubs

Seeking a Balance

Sometimes minority students (especially students of color and gay, lesbian, and bisexual students) feel both internal and external pressure to affiliate almost exclusively with their relevant minority community and, in the process, neglect connections with the mainstream, nonminority community. In the eyes of some in the minority community, a lack of total commitment is a sign of "selling out" or of being ashamed of your heritage, background, or sexual identity. As a minority student, you need to start thinking about how much of a commitment you are willing to make and how you will deal with students who question your level of commitment.

Remember that you are not playing an all-or-nothing game. You can affiliate with your relevant minority community and not totally disconnect yourself from the larger mainstream community. In seeking a balance, you may find a profound sense of belonging in the minority community, without losing the benefits of friends, organizations, and activities unrelated to your minority status.

Self-Segregation

Self-segregation can occur in class (sitting by other minority students), in the dining halls (eating at all-minority tables), and in the residences (choosing a minority roommate or living in a fraternity or sorority). Often students self-segregate without even realizing they are doing it. Of course, there is nothing wrong with self-segregation. Being with others like ourselves can help us to understand and define our identity and provide comfort during the often-stressful college years.

However, a large part of the college experience is meeting and getting to know a large variety of people. Self-segregation obviously has the potential to limit your ability to know and understand a wider spectrum of individuals. As you decide where you are going to live and who you will spend your time with, be cognizant of the advantages and disadvantages of self-segregation.

66 *There is no such thing as self-segregation. And, if there is, discussion of it should not be confined to the behavior of minorities. Why are blacks and other minorities considered to be self-segregating when the majority group is doing the same thing in larger numbers? Perhaps minorities are viewed as self-segregating because they're easier to identify. In other words, it's easier to point out five members of a minority group sitting at a lunchroom table than to notice the 500 members of the majority group 'self-segregating' in the rest of the cafeteria."*

—Calvin Gladney, Cornell University

Dealing with Controversial and Difficult Issues

66 *A group of us were talking and a friend told an anti-Semitic joke. I am not even sure he realized his story was anti-Semitic. But I felt uncomfortable. I think everyone around me felt a little uncomfortable. I told him that, as a Jew, I was offended by his remarks. He actually thanked me for explaining my feelings. It's one thing hearing a minority person telling a joke about his or her particular minority group; it's quite another to hear the story from someone who is not a member of that group. I'm glad I said something."*

—Gloria Brown, University of California, Berkeley

During your college years, be prepared to hear racist remarks on campus (and perhaps even in the classroom) and to see offensive literature. Sometimes a racist remark or offensive literature can precipitate a university-wide forum to discuss the issue of diversity on campus. Other times such events spark organized discussions within your minority community. In many cases, however, there will be no major outcry. You will need to decide how you want to address the situation—by yourself or with a small group of peers. For example, you may be eating dinner with a group of friends and someone will say something that offends you. Realize that there is no "right" way to respond. Some people feel comfortable confronting the individual right there. Others prefer not to say anything and simply avoid that individual. Your reactions may change over time and may depend on the situation and your relationship with the individual in question.

Racist behavior based on hate, as opposed to misunderstanding, should not be tolerated. If you are deeply offended by what another student (or even a professor) has said, you should feel free to bring your concerns to the attention of older students, your adviser, or the relevant administrator at your college. Most schools treat such behavior very seriously. It's probably a good idea not to try to solve the situation by yourself. Ask an older student or someone you trust for advice on how to handle the incident.

Differences Within Your Minority Community

Like any other group of people, a minority group will have its tensions, differences, and divisions. Invariably, someone will fall into the minority, even in a minority group. For example, you may be a conservative in an African-American community that is traditionally liberal or a feminist in a minority group not known for progressive views about women. There is nothing wrong with having different views, but you may want to think about how you will respond to others who question your beliefs. Most students respect differences of opinion that are based on honest reflection and sincere conviction. You may even inspire discussion within your minority community about some of these differences. Constructive, and sometimes heated, discussion is part of what makes college a meaningful and worthwhile experience.

Intersectionality

"Intersectionality" is the term modern scholars of ethnicity, gender, and sexual orientation use to describe the phenomenon of simultaneously being a member of multiple minority groups. In other words, many minority students find themselves at the "intersection" of different minority identities. For example, you may be an African-American female or an individual who is both Latino and gay.

If you are in this position, do not despair. Many universities have student groups at the various intersections of minority identities. For example, your school may have an organization for gay, lesbian, and bisexual students of color. Some minority communities have their own organizations that acknowledge the intersection of identity. For example, the African-American, Asian American, and Latino communities may each have their own organizations for women or gay and lesbian students. Many university women's centers have organizations for lesbian and bisexual women.

In addition to these intersectional groups, you also have the option of associating with several different minority groups. For example, an African-American woman who is bisexual might find herself working with her university's African-American theater organization; helping to organize the next gay, lesbian, and bisexual dance; and staffing the university's women's center. Once again, you are not playing an all-or-nothing game. If you are an intersectional minority, you should seek out the people, the organizations, and the activities that make you feel the most comfortable and that add the most joy and meaning to your life—regardless of the demographics.

Making an Academic Pursuit Out of Your Minority Identity

66 *Combining my study of English literature with a second major in the history of African-American music was one of the most personally and academically fulfilling things I ever did. I learned a lot about the place of music in African-American culture and the importance of African-American music to broader American culture."*

—Martina Stewart, Yale University

College often represents your first opportunity to choose classes and an academic major. It also will be the first time you will have access to classes that focus specifically on minority groups and the minority experience. Many universities have full programs and departments in African-American, Asian, Asian American, Latino, Latin American, and women's studies. Some universities even have programs in Native American studies and gay, lesbian, and bisexual studies.

Any student can take classes in these areas. Minority students, however, may feel particularly drawn to these fields of study. Some minority students are so excited about the opportunity to learn more about their culture, history, and traditions that they choose to major in a type of minority studies. Other minority students shy away from concentrating in these areas, perhaps because they are not "traditional" areas of study.

If you are interested in minority studies, you should try a class early on to see if it whets your appetite. If it does, you might want to consider majoring in that area or combining that interest with a more traditional field of study, such as history or biology. Many students focus on a more traditional area of study around their interest in minority studies. For example, you could major in history with a concentration in African-American history. Other students choose to double major, sometimes in two drastically different areas, such as Latin American studies and biology. Double majoring is not easy. You may need to plan your course work carefully from the very beginning to graduate in four years.

A Final Bit of Advice

During your college years, you will spend a lot of time thinking about who you are and who you want to become. As a minority student, you might want to consider how your minority identity plays a role in shaping how you define yourself. As you make choices about what to study, who to live with, and who to spend time with, remember that this process of self-definition belongs to you and to you alone. Don't feel pressured to be who you think others in your minority community or in the wider, mainstream community want you to be. Be true to the only person you really need to answer to—yourself.

CHAPTER 15

Greek versus Dorm Life

66 *Going Greek was one of the best decisions I've made since coming to college.*

Especially at a big school, it's often hard to find your place. You're on your own for the first time. You don't know anyone. You miss being around things that make you comfortable.

But the Greek system can make a big school so much smaller. It offers you a house full of friends that most likely will stay with you for the rest of your life. It gives you a renewed sense of comfort because you are around people who are like you and who have chosen you to be in their group. It doesn't take away from your studies either; in fact, it helped me because many of my sisters were in the same classes, and we studied together in groups.

Also, if you're talking about fun, the Greek system gives you an active social life, which no dormitory experience can hope to match."

—Susan Yates, Washington State University

❝ *The Greek system is a big thing at my school, but I didn't think I needed it.*

To me, the Greek system is a social crutch. It's for people who can't make it on their own. Greeks hang around people that are exactly alike.

But isn't that the antithesis of what college is supposed to be about? College is supposed to be about meeting new people—people who you maybe didn't come into contact with during high school. It's a time to learn about new ideas. The Greek system won't provide that.

The dorms, on the other hand, have allowed me to meet a wide variety of people, given me just enough partying, and provided a good study environment. For me, the choice was easy."

—Brian Graham, Lafayette College

What Did Plato Think?

Plato, one of the original Greeks, envisaged a society where justice was founded on moral absolutes. While today's Greek system falls slightly short of Plato's utopia, it still uses the same alphabet. It also provides an excellent housing alternative for many college students.

However, most incoming students opt for school-sponsored dormitories and choose to live in dorms that are single sex, coed by room, or coed by floor.

Although this chapter cannot pretend to make the choice between becoming Greek or staying in the dorms, it will illuminate the differences surrounding these two living arrangements. Following are the answers to the most common questions regarding Greek versus dormitory life.

Some Common Questions

1. HOW DO HOUSING ARRANGEMENTS DIFFER?

Dorms: Typical accommodations consist of two people sharing a room. Each dorm floor has one or two community bathrooms, depending on whether the floor is single sex or coed. The typical dorm also may have a dining hall, television room, a mail room, study cubicles, a pay phone, and a laundry facility.

Greeks: Most fraternities and sororities are based in large houses. Denoted by two or three letters of the Greek alphabet (such as Sigma Alpha Epsilon or Alpha Epsilon Pi), most Greek houses or "chapters" are located close to each other, sometimes on a street known as Greek Row.

As in the dorms, you may have to share a room. Even worse, many Greeks are forced to sleep on sleeping porches, which house about thirty students in one large room full of bunk beds. If you are sleeping on the porch, you may have to keep your clothes in another part of the house and commute back and forth.

Like the dormitories, Greek houses have dining halls, television rooms, mail rooms, study rooms, pay phones, a laundry facility, and a "party area" as well.

 Psst . . . Because of housing shortages, some colleges (UC Berkeley, for example) may require students to find off-campus housing, even during their freshman year. The housing office at your school usually has a list of apartments and homes available to students. One good reason to go Greek is that your fraternity or sorority undoubtedly will provide affordable housing.

2. WHAT ABOUT FOOD?

Dorms: If you are on a school meal plan, count on eating two to three meals a day in a specified cafeteria. Some meal plans, however, allow you to dine in a variety of campus cafeterias, each with a different style of food (Mexican, Italian, etc.). Check out the meal options, paying special attention to the number of meals you are allotted and the stipulations on your plan. If you sign up to eat twenty-plus meals a week, remember that you will have to get up for every breakfast—and that's often when the roosters are crowing—and rarely have the option of eating out. Signing up for fourteen meals a week may be more prudent.

Greeks: Most Greek chapters have cooks who make all the meals. The quality of food, therefore, is contingent on the ability of the cook. Depending on the student, taste buds may play a slight role in determining which houses you rush.

3. DO LIVING COSTS DIFFER?

Dorms: Although tuition fluctuates from college to college, housing costs remain relatively the same. Regardless of whether you are in a fraternity or dorm, expect to pay at least $1,500 per semester for room and board.

Greeks: A common misconception is that Greeks pay more for housing because they have so many social functions. Fraternities and sororities are able to keep living costs low and still have a multitude of social gatherings because members perform many of the household chores otherwise taken care of by paid employees. Greeks often wash dishes, clean the bathrooms, and make physical repairs themselves.

4. WHAT IS THE PROCEDURE FOR JOINING?

Dorms: You sign up, you pay, you're in. Actually, it's not quite that simple.

Many colleges allow you to request specific dorms. Ask upperclassmen from your hometown about the differences between the dormitories on campus. Some are better than others.

Many colleges also give you the opportunity to select coed, single-sex, all-freshmen, or four-class dormitories.

Greeks: Joining a fraternity or sorority is slightly more complicated than signing up for a dormitory. Instead of choosing a place to live, a student must be invited to join the Greek system.

This invitation to join, called a "bid," must be approved by a large majority of the sorority or fraternity members. Bids are given out following a period called "rush."

Although it may seem that the fraternities and sororities do most of the "choosing," this is certainly not the case. You, in effect, do most of the "choosing" by deciding which houses you wish to rush and which houses you wish to ignore.

Rush takes place during the summer at some schools; in this case, you might have "pledged" (or chosen to join) a fraternity or sorority before you even begin your freshman year. At other universities, rush takes place during the school year.

Various colleges handle rush differently. At many schools, the women go through formal rush and visit every sorority before deciding on which one they wish to pledge. Men, however, usually get to choose which fraternities they want to rush without looking at all the houses. Although you can join only one house, you can rush as many as you wish.

Those students who receive a bid to join a fraternity or sorority must go through a pledge period before they become members. During this pledge period, the pledges are expected to perform various tasks for the "actives," the members of the house. These tasks usually are given with good intentions. The pledges may be asked to clean dishes or rake the lawn. Sometimes, however, the tasks can be abusive; this is called "hazing." Hazing is illegal at all schools, and fraternities and sororities can be severely punished for this type of pledging.

5. HOW DOES THE SOCIAL LIFE DIFFER?

Dorms: You have a lot more control over your social life in the dormitories than you do as a Greek. Although your dormitory will undoubtedly throw parties and have meetings, your attendance at these events is never mandatory. The events are simply put on for those who wish to attend them.

66 *During my first year of college before I transferred, I attended the University of Washington, a state school with a large, influential Greek system. At the beginning of the year I went through rush and joined the Tri-Delts. Although I lived at the sorority, I had several friends who lived in dorms and who were not socially affiliated with the Greek system.*

As I became more familiar with the social life of a dormie, I noticed it didn't seem much different from the social life of a Greek. Each held weekly meetings, threw parties, sponsored study breaks, and planned off-campus excursions.

In spite of the similarities, a considerable number of dormies were adamantly opposed to the Greeks. We are talking total resentment— almost fanatical. Their criticism must have been directed toward something other than Greek social life because dorm social life was essentially the same."

—Leslie Friend, University of Chicago

In the simplest of terms, you make your own social life in the dorms. You can go to as many parties as you like, or you can study until the Red Sea parts again.

Greeks: It is much easier to have an active social life in the Greek system. There are more parties, more functions with other fraternities and sororities, and, most importantly, a more "social" crowd. In addition, your attendance at many of these events is mandatory or, at least, strongly suggested.

Being in a fraternity or sorority also puts you in a more "social" scene. For example, it is quite common for a fraternity brother or sorority sister to set you up on a date with one of their Greek friends.

6. WHAT IS AN UNHOUSED FRATERNITY OR SORORITY?

Along with a housed Greek system, some campuses have unhoused fraternities and sororities. These unhoused Greeks hold meetings in a specified area on campus each week. Their members may live in the dorms or off campus.

Unhoused Greeks claim they have the best of both worlds. The students can intermix with the variety of men and women found in the dorms, while still maintaining many of the bonds formed in a fraternity or sorority.

Greeks versus Dorms: Advantages and Disadvantages

66 *I was ambivalent about joining a fraternity at first. Then I thought about it: Why am I going to college in the first place? Is it because of the degree? Partly . . . but I could get a degree at night school, if I was that desperate.*

Is it because of the teachers? Partly . . . but teachers, no matter how good, certainly don't justify the huge amount of money I'm dishing out for tuition. So, why? Why am I going to college? I think the main reason for going to college is the other students you meet.

A fraternity, for all its negatives, is a great way to meet fifty new guys who, in a lot of ways, are a lot like you. My best friends are in my fraternity. And they will be my friends for the rest of my life.

No matter how you look at it, that's a whole bunch of guys who are going to be your business contacts, your tennis partners, your whatever-you-want-them-to-be. That's a big part of what college should be about."

—Greg Gottesman, Stanford University

❝ *If you're not in the Greek system at a big school like the University of Washington, you basically have to work really hard just to have a social life."*

—Katie MacDonald, University of Washington

❝ *I went through rush and pledged a sorority but found the whole thing to be too fake. After we were initiated as pledges, my newfound sisters immediately began crying and telling each other how they were all best friends now.*

We were all holding these candles in a dark room and each girl would tell the whole group her deepest and darkest secrets. Then she would cry and thank everybody for letting her bond with the sorority. But I couldn't help thinking, 'I don't even know these people and I'm supposed to tell them my deepest and darkest secrets.'

For some, that's great, but sorority life wasn't for me."

—Pam Brown, San Diego State University

❝ *Coming from out of state, I was apprehensive going to UCLA because I didn't really know anybody. Joining a fraternity gave me a place to belong."*

—Tim Eng, UCLA

In a nutshell, a fraternity or sorority is going to give you a more active social life and a closer-knit group of friends. Your time will be more regimented, but most of the activities you participate in will be enjoyable. The most often-heard complaint about Greeks is that they tend to be superficial, caring only about their fraternity and/or sorority and not about other things affecting the college community or the world.

A dormitory will allow you more freedom than a Greek house. You will live with a wider variety of people, including both men and women. The friends you make, however, probably will not be as long lasting as those made in the Greek system, nor will you have the fellowship that the Greek system fosters.

Ten Basic Considerations of Greek Versus Dorm Life

As you have read, there are advantages and disadvantages to both Greek and dorm life. Following are ten considerations that may help you to form a clearer opinion as to where you stand in the Greek-versus-dorm picture.

1. Greeks live in an all-male or an all-female environment. Dormitories can be coed. Which would you prefer?
   ❐   Greeks
   ❐   Dorms

2. Greeks usually do things together; their activities center on large groups. Those in the dorms do more things individually or in very small groups. Which would you prefer?
   ❐   Greeks
   ❐   Dorms

3. Greeks usually decide what activities and charities to support as a group. You are expected to back the group's decision. In a dorm, your decisions as to what you support will be mostly your own. Which would you prefer?
   ❐   Greeks
   ❐   Dorms

4. Greeks usually have their time more regimented. Greeks are expected to perform house duties and the like. In a dorm, your time will be less regimented. Which would you prefer?
   ❐   Greeks
   ❐   Dorms

5. Greeks tend to be homogeneous. They choose people who they think will fit in well with the group. This usually makes for a spirited environment. In the dorms, there are more people from different countries, religions, races, and socioeconomic backgrounds. Which would you prefer?
   ❐   Greeks
   ❐   Dorms

6. During the pledge period (usually one quarter), the Greeks demand a huge amount of time from their pledges. Although you undoubtedly will have fun, you may have to sacrifice some study time. The dorms have nothing like this. Which would you prefer?

☐   Greeks

☐   Dorms

7. If you plan on becoming a Greek, are you prepared to meet rejection? Many times you won't receive a bid from the house you wanted; it's possible that you may not receive a bid from any house at all. The dorms have nothing like this. Which would you prefer?

☐   Greeks

☐   Dorms

8. In the Greek system, you will determine who you live with and actually vote on who you think should be in your house the upcoming year. In the dorms, you live with people who are randomly selected. Which would you prefer?

☐   Greeks

☐   Dorms

9. Greeks usually provide their members with an active social life. In the dorms, you are more individually responsible for your social life. Which would you prefer?

☐   Greeks

☐   Dorms

10. Greeks tend to keep their fraternal or sororal ties long after college is over. This may lead to business contacts or just friends in different areas of the country. Although you can make close friendships in the dorms, the long-lasting ties are usually harder to maintain. Which would you prefer?

☐   Greeks

☐   Dorms

The Big Question: Should You Rush?

If you have any questions about whether you should rush, do it. You can always back out later.

Still, don't go into rush with your heart pinned to your sleeve. The rush process is not perfect. It favors the more outgoing and the more physically attractive. Actives make decisions on first impressions. The system is, at best, superficial. Keep this in mind and be prepared to face rejection.

❝ *I would encourage everyone to rush. Even if you are not planning on pledging a fraternity or sorority, rush is probably the best time you will have to meet people and make new friends.*

But be prepared to face rejection! I had a friend who was dying to be in the Greek system, but she was rejected by all four of the sororities that she wanted to get into. She was extremely hurt. It's hard not to take that sort of rejection personally."

—Pam Brown, San Diego State University

Last but Not Least: Be Yourself!

Regardless of whether you are rushing a fraternity or sorority or planning on living in the dorms, remember to be yourself.

A lot of people will rush a fraternity or sorority and act totally different than they otherwise would. For example, a guy may get drunk every night, even though he hates drinking. This only leads to problems later when the people in your fraternity or sorority expect you to act a certain way and you don't want to.

As previous chapters in this book have suggested, other students probably will like you more for who you are than who you pretend to be.

CHAPTER 16

Laundry and Ironing

Laundry

Directions for washing:

1. *Fill cap to line for normal load.*

2. *For tough spots and stains, pour detergent directly on soiled areas and rub in.*

3. *For hand-washing delicate fabrics, add a little detergent to each gallon of water, then add item(s). Soak briefly, wash gently, then rinse thoroughly.*

These washing instructions, delectable in their simplicity, could seemingly be followed by any Neanderthal.

Ah, but judge not lest ye be judged.

In reality, laundry can be a most difficult endeavor, as witnessed by the foibles of one college freshman. This frosh learned the hard way one of life's most important lessons: Never put reds with anything even remotely white.

❝ *Here I was, content with my whites in one neat pile and my darks in another. So, I scrambled down to the washing machines in the dormitory basement and carefully put my whites in two of the machines and my darks in two others. I put in the correct amount of detergent as per the instructions on the box and deposited the required number of quarters.*

As I walked back into my room upstairs, I was aghast to see that I had forgotten to wash my red Stanford sweatshirt. I grabbed it and ran down to the basement. The machines with the darks were already too full. You usually end up with more darks because of blue jeans, towels, and stuff. Feeling pretty confident that enough time remained in order to fully cleanse my sweatshirt, I threw it into one of the machines with white clothes. I was pretty sure the red on the sweatshirt would not bleed. I had already washed it twice before.

The rest is history. I have been wearing pink underwear, socks, T-shirts, and sleeping in pink sheets ever since.

Let me say one thing before parting. You can totally mess up a midterm in college. You can forget your coat at a frat party. You can even date your roommate's old sweetheart, if you're daring. But never, ever, wash your reds with your whites.❞

—Greg Gottesman, Stanford University

The Twelve Commandments

Hopefully, this story will save you from the pink reign many college students face in their freshman year. Of course, "not putting reds in with the whites" is only one of the many rules of laundering and ironing. To keep you out of trouble, *College Survival* has consulted a few laundromats, tailors, and moms for a list of basic tenets. The twelve commandments read as follows:

1. READ THE LABELS ON YOUR CLOTHES.

Poor Katie MacDonald. During her freshman year at Washington, she was forced to send home her newly purchased—and newly washed—ski sweater to her seven-year-old cousin. Alas, it was even too small for the seven-year-old, and it became the pride of Katie's dog, Mugger.

Dear Katie, she should have read the label, which would have succinctly told her that 100 percent wool sweaters are not machine washable (except for certain types, which are tagged as "machine washable"). She could have done it by hand in cold water or sent it to the local cleaners.

You don't have to be a Katie. Thanks to the Federal Trade Commission (FTC), all garments must have care instructions. For example, the label inside a sweater must tell you if the garment is machine washable, 100 percent cotton, and so on.

When packing for college, consider easy-care fabrics. There won't be time at school to hand-wash your rayon.

2. MAKE SURE YOU HAVE ENOUGH QUARTERS BEFORE BEGINNING YOUR LOAD.

In high school, quarters are like any other medium of exchange; they are worth no more than two dimes and a nickel. In college, however, quarters assume monumental significance. Ryan Drant, a junior at Stanford University, used to maintain a "special" quarters cup. No one was allowed near it.

You're probably wondering why quarters are so sacred? . . . well, just about everything at college requires quarters. Caffeinated soda for that all-night paper . . . candy and gum for that 3-hour seminar . . . and, yes, washers and dryers.

Don't be the hall beggar. When you go to the bank, remember to request a few rolls of quarters. Ask for them when you're at the grocery store. Bring some from home. And, heaven forbid, don't go down the three flights of stairs without several in hand. Dryers and washers usually require three or four quarters apiece. Taking into account that you will be using about three washers and two dryers per "usual ten-day" laundry load, 15 or more quarters should suffice. Not cheap!

Some schools have introduced a way of paying for your laundry electronically. In this case, you deposit a certain amount of money into an account at the beginning of the year and then use a card or a code to access that account from the laundry room and pay for your laundry. If your school has such a system, it's probably a good idea to take advantage of it—that is, if you don't like begging or searching for quarters!

3. CHECK YOUR POCKETS.

"I wish I had a dime for every dollar my mom found in my jeans before washing them." That was Aristotle, wasn't it?

There are some things that you do not want as sparkling clean as your everyday duds. Your wallet, for starters. Your syllabus from your first anthropology class. Your calculus assignment. A picture of your new girlfriend. Gum.

So, do what mom has done for years: Empty your pockets before washing. It only takes a second—and it can save hours of pulling Kleenex fluff off your clothes.

4. ALWAYS SEPARATE DARKS AND LIGHTS.

This commandment includes the all-important separation of reds and whites. If you thought we were going to beat this dead dog into the ground, you were pretty much on target. But in all seriousness, remember this rule. If you think some article of clothing is dark (and it might run), don't put it into the load with whites. For example, blue jeans and *colored* collegiate sweatshirts are *dark*. Believe it . . . new Levi's have colored more underwear than Fruit of the Loom.

5. USE PRE-WASH ON "STUBBORN" STAINS.

No, most college freshman do not have a ready supply of pre-wash in their room. Then again, a good number of college freshman do not care that much about "stubborn" stains. So, this one is up to you. If you like your clothes the way they were meant to be worn (without spots), get a bottle or stick of pre-wash for a few bucks. Spray your smudges with the pre-wash and throw the article in with the rest of your clothes.

6. SET THE MACHINE ON COLD OR WARM WATER TEMPERATURE—NOT HOT.

Most detergents today are made to work well in all water temperatures. According to most moms and professional launderers, however, the "hot water" setting on commercial machines should never be trusted. Not only will hot water aid your dark clothes in bleeding all over their lighter peers, but it also will play a role in shrinking a major part of your wardrobe.

Commercial machines are set differently than home ones. The "hot" setting on commercial machines may be akin to hellfire. Cold or warm water is always safer.

7. NEVER OVERLOAD THE MACHINES.

Big mistake. Sure, it is not going to kill the machine if you put a few extra socks in—but don't add a few extra towels. Almost every freshman hears about one notorious washing machine explosion before the end of the first year. Spend the extra 75¢ or you might be swimming in it.

8. READ THE INSTRUCTIONS ON THE DETERGENT BOX.

Make sure to read the instructions on how much detergent to add to the load. When in doubt, it is better to use too little rather than too much. Too much soap can leave film on your clothes. It also can irritate your skin. Usually instructions will tell you to add a cup of powdered detergent. If a measuring cup does not come with the box, buy one. It's a pain to play the how-much-detergent-equals-a-cup game each laundry session. You can use the cap to measure liquid detergents. Premeasured tablets and packets are easier to use than liquids or powders, but they cost more, too.

9. USE BLEACH WISELY AND, OF COURSE, ONLY WITH WHITES.

Even though it is cheap, bleach is the rich man's washing tool. In other words, you don't really need it. Granted, it makes your whites whiter, but many college freshman run out of bleach and never feel like spending the extra money to replace it. Nevertheless, it can be helpful when employed correctly. Use it only when washing white clothes. (Or, for colors, you may decide to use a separate color-safe bleach, or a detergent with color-safe bleach included—but it's generally not necessary for keeping colored fabric clean.) Also, remember to put it in the designated dispenser or to add it after the water has completely filled the machine. Roger, an owner of a Laundromat in Seattle, warns, "Do not pour bleach directly onto your clothes or you might burn a hole right through them."

In addition, bleach—when overused—has a tendency to weaken the fibers in your clothes, causing many articles in your wardrobe to become hole-infested at a faster rate.

So, until huge holes in odd places come back in style, use bleach wisely.

10. TURN YOUR PATTERNED CLOTHES AND SWEATERS INSIDE OUT BEFORE WASHING.

Ah, the mysteries of laundering!

After the end of their first quarter, many freshmen find the designs on their T-shirts fading. If they only knew what others across the nation have known for years . . . that is, turn your patterned garments inside out. By doing this, colors stay intense and designs intact.

Also, if you machine wash any of your sweaters, turn them inside out too, that way the little balls of fuzz will form on the inside, not the outside.

11. WATCH THE TIME TO AVOID THEFT.

Woe to the guy or gal who finds the kid in his calculus class wearing his favorite sweater. Indeed, theft is the favorite subject among many college students and also among local thieves.

When it comes to theft, the washing machines are just about the easiest prey around. College students tend to let their clothes sit for hours while they read that next chapter, watch the fourth quarter of Monday Night Football, kiss their new boyfriend ten extra times, or catch up on a little shut-eye. Next thing you know . . . K-Mart here I come!

Many college students avoid theft by sitting in the laundry room and doing homework while their clothes wash and dry. For those impatient ones, setting a timer and making sure to pick up the clothes as soon as they are finished makes sense. Besides, leaving your clothes in the drier or washing machine after the time has expired is unfair to others wishing to use the machines.

You also should leave a laundry basket (with your name on it) on top of the washer or drier in question. Not only will this encourage your dormmates to put your clothes in a clean basket instead of on the dirty floor, but it also will facilitate carrying your clothes up two or three flights of stairs.

12. FOLD YOUR CLOTHES AS SOON AS THEY LEAVE THE DRIER.

This hint should allow you to bypass most ironing.

For some reason (unknown to science), wrinkles and the time immediately after clothes leave the drier are directly proportional. If you fold your clothes as soon as they leave the drier, you will be assured of fewer wrinkles and spiffy-looking duds. It only takes a few minutes and will save you hours of ironing.

Yes, You Can Avoid Steps 1–12, But . . .

Many schools have a laundry service for students. For a certain amount of money per semester (and sometimes it is pretty expensive), students can drop off their laundry once a week and pick it up the next day.

❝ *While the school laundry service saves a valuable amount of time and energy, its quality should not be mistaken for top notch. Luckily, I myself have never been unfortunate enough to lose a favorite shirt or pair of jeans. However, early in my freshman year, I found in my returned bag of clothes not just my boxers and T-shirts, but a good portion of someone else's wardrobe as well. Being the Good Samaritan that I am, I was able to track the poor guy down after a few days (though he admittedly showed up in my room wearing a sticky pair of underwear and without socks). Ever since then, I've been careful not to put my best clothes in the school laundry bag, instead opting to free-ride and add them to a friend's self-washed laundry load."*

—Aaron R. Cohen, Harvard University

The advantage of this system is that your laundry will definitely get done once a week (assuming you remember to drop it off), which is far more often than most college students who do their own laundry get around to it. And of course it means that you don't have to do any work. But the disadvantages include not only the price, which is guaranteed to be much steeper than if you did your own wash, but also the fact that you can't really tell the laundry service that you want your new shirt from grandma to line dry or that you want those favorite pants to come out of the drier 10 minutes early so they don't shrink. Laundry services are great at socks, underwear, T-shirts, and jeans — they just chuck it all in a washer and then chuck it all in a drier, but if you have special procedures for particular items of clothing, forget it; you're better off doing it yourself.

Ironing

T.J. Burke, a student from the University of San Diego, claims the worst thing about freshman year was the "wrinkles"—not from stress, not from age, not from sun. "Nope!" T.J. said. "It was those darn laundry wrinkles."

T.J. admits he should have learned how to wield an iron. And after some research, T.J. gave us six helpful hints.

1. KEEP THE BOTTOM OF THE IRON CLEAN.

You have washed your shirt. Looks great. You iron it. Even better.

But wait! What are those spots doing on your perfect shirt?

Oops, the bottom of your iron must have been dirty. It could have been soil from your floor or starch build-up.

Just know that, during iron use, any debris on the bottom of the iron will become firmly implanted in your garment. So, keep the bottom clean. Tissue paper will work. If that does not solve your problem, many experts recommend cleaning your iron with a light grade of steel wool.

2. IRON ON TOP OF A TOWEL.

66 *It seemed simple enough. I had some serious wrinkle build-up, so I went down the hall, borrowed an iron, and got to work. My blue-shag carpet seemed like a good place to set the shirt, so that's where I started to iron.*

It was one of my best shirts. I'm using the past tense for a reason, of course. When I picked up the shirt, I had implanted most of the carpet onto the back of it—blue-shag carpet! I guess it must have been the heat from the iron. I never could get out all the carpet, but the shirt worked great for one of those '70s dances. You work with what you have."

—Ed Malakoff, Brown University

If you don't have a smooth, clean surface on which to iron, make sure to set down a towel, preferably a white one.

At college, you won't have room to store a full-size ironing board. Improvise effectively. There are mini, desk-top ironing boards for sale for about $20 at many stores around college campuses. Barring that, a clean desk with a few white towels covering it is probably your best bet.

3. LIGHTLY SPRAY YOUR CLOTHES WITH WATER, SIZING, OR SPRAY STARCH BEFORE IRONING.

Have you ever ironed a shirt for an hour? Have you ever ironed a shirt for an hour and still had those awful wrinkles staring you in the face?

Spray starch, for a just a few bucks, is a miracle. It will save you time and give your clothes that professionally "pressed" look. In addition, spray starch will give your clothes extra body.

Sizing, which is located next to spray starch in the grocery store, may be even better. Apparently, this fabric relaxant gives you all the benefits of spray starch without causing starch build-up.

If spray starch or sizing is not available, water will get out most of the creases; still, water will not give your clothes body or that "crisp" look.

Silks and certain delicate fabrics should not be sprayed with starch, sizing, or water. Take delicate fabrics to the cleaners. Pressing a formal dress is usually not a good idea . . . let the pros handle it.

4. KNOW YOUR IRON.

Make sure to check your clothing to find out what it is made of before you start ironing. If you try to iron rayon on the linen setting you will have a melted plastic ball when you're done. If you try linen on the rayon setting, the iron won't be hot enough to get out the wrinkles. Make sure that your iron is set to match your fabric. If your iron simply has numbers, follow this guide:

1—Acetate and Acrylic

2—Nylon and Silk

3—Polyester and Rayon

4—Cotton Blends (60/40 Cotton/Polyester, etc.)

5—Wool

6—Cotton

7—Linen

A steam iron is your best bet. If you have a dry iron, however, use it on the medium setting—not on hot! The hot setting on a dry iron may stick to your fabric, scorch, and possibly melt it.

A steam iron, on the other hand, is more forgiving. Haruko Yaguchi, a tailor for the past forty years, uses a steam iron on even the most expensive garments. She gives a word of caution: Some areas in the country have "hard" water. In these areas, fill your steam iron with distilled water. This will increase the longevity of your appliance and decrease the chance of residue building on the bottom of your machine.

5. IRON THE COLLAR AND CUFFS FIRST.

Thankfully, there is a method to this madness called ironing. If you do not want anemic-looking garments after three or four rounds of pressing, iron your shirts in this order: (1) the collar, (2) the cuffs, (3) the sleeves, (4) the back, and (5) the front. Of course, you should iron the most important part of your garment last.

Once you have mastered the shirt, you can apply this method in various forms to the rest of your wardrobe.

6. DON'T FORGET TO TURN OFF THE IRON WHEN NOT IN USE.

66 *I was ironing one of my favorite shirts one day when the phone rang. Usually I'm careful about turning off the iron before I get into other things. But this time I forgot, to say the least.*

It was a long-distance call—an old friend from home. We started talking and one of my hands just kind of left the iron sitting on the shirt.

Ten minutes later I looked down and the shirt had a six-inch hole in it. The iron burned right through the shirt.

If it was a pair of jeans, I could have turned them into shorts. But, in this case, I would have been exposing something I usually like to keep hidden. I always remember to turn off the iron now."

—Jessica Weinman, UC-Santa Barbara

This tip is self-explanatory. Irons are hot. Really hot. If you don't turn off your iron by mistake, chances are you will be calling the local fire department. So, it's simple: Don't forget.

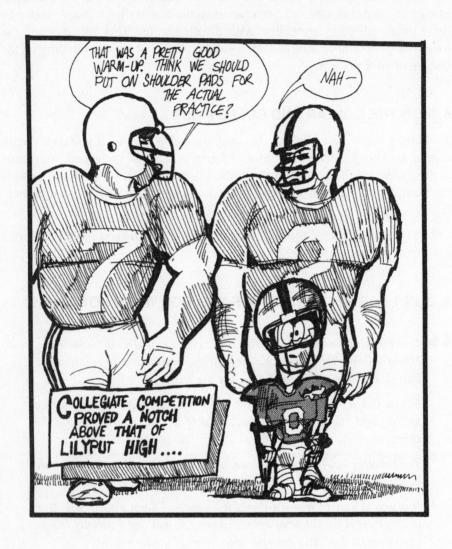

CHAPTER 17

Athletics and Exercise: Varsity to Intramural

66 *People always ask me how I can let varsity tennis take so much of my time. They tell me how meaningless it is to hit a little yellow fuzzy thing over the net. 'What about education? What about girls? What about fun?' they ask.*

'What about fun?' I respond. First, there is nothing I like better than a competitive three-set match in the heat of the day. Second, while others are relieving stress through unneeded Z's or hops and barley, I can always count on a good practice to ease my mind. Third, where education is concerned, I have this motto: 'Strong mind, strong body.' A healthy body allows you to concentrate harder and study more efficiently. Finally, as far as girls are concerned, they love guys in tennis shorts."

—Keith Vernon, University of Puget Sound

Should You Participate?

If you ever played a sport in high school, if you ever got together with some friends for a game of two-hand touch, if you ever went jogging—heck, if you ever took a walk in a park, athletics and/or exercise should play some role in your collegiate experience. Anything is better than lethargy!

Even if you are not planning on playing a varsity sport, the least you should do is join an intramural team, jog, walk, or take an aerobics class. Exercising regularly contributes to better health and allows the mind to think more clearly.

What Sports Do Colleges Offer?

Colleges offer almost every sport imaginable on some level (whether varsity, club, or intramural). Baseball. Basketball. Football. Tennis. Swimming. Soccer. Lacrosse. Wind surfing. Fencing. Tae Kwon Do. Chess?

If the school does not provide your desired sport, finding an interested group of guys and girls is never difficult, especially at larger schools.

What About Varsity Sports?

66 *We had two individuals on our team who each played less than two years of high school soccer. They both walked on. Neither was all-state or all-league in high school. Yet, they graduated as four-year starters on a women's soccer team that was ranked in the top five in the nation. Both of them were captains of the team. One of them was an All-American."*

—Colleen Hacker, Soccer Coach, Pacific Lutheran University

Comparing high school athletics to college athletics is like comparing a paper airplane to an F-15. Students who don't realize the difference are leaving the door open to disappointment.

Colleen Hacker, the women's soccer coach at Pacific Lutheran University, insists that students be realistic in assessing their athletic ability. "Simply being the star on your high school team does not guarantee success at the college level," she said.

Nevertheless, the high level of competition should not discourage those who are interested from trying out. Be realistic—but never sell yourself short.

How Do I Get Involved?

Sign-up procedures depend on your school. Varsity coaches have office hours; go in and speak with them if you are interested. Try-out times for various varsity sports are easily accessible.

For intramural and club sports, most colleges have a recreation office where students can sign up. Dormitories and Greek houses often post sign-up lists as well. Some universities even give credit for those participating in school-sponsored sports—varsity to intramural. Talk about believing in the strong mind, strong body concept!

The Myths Surrounding College Athletics

Myths pervade college athletics. Recruiting and drug scandals fill newspaper headlines. Other stories of students graduating without knowing how to read or write warp the public's view of the true nature of college sports.

The next section clears up three common myths.

MYTH #1: YOU DON'T HAVE THE TIME TO PLAY.

Many freshmen heading off to college think they won't have time to breathe, let alone play a sport. Wrong!

The wonderful thing about college is that you will have more free time than ever before. Approximately 3 hours a day will be spent in class; the rest is yours. You are not going to study the entire other 21 hours, and, even with a part-time job, you still will have plenty of free time.

More explicitly, time should not be an excuse for abandoning exercise—at any level.

If you are a varsity NCAA Division I athlete (depending on the sport and season), expect to spend 3 to 6 hours practicing a day. For example, during football season, Division I teams demand about 6 hours, including time on the field and in the training room.

Division II, Division III, and NAIA athletes spend less time on the field. During each athlete's respective season, 2 to 4 hours of practice a day is standard. In these divisions, more emphasis is placed on academic as opposed to athletic success.

MYTH #2: THE ONLY "REAL" COMPETITION TAKES PLACE IN DIVISION I.

When one thinks of college sports, Division I teams like Oklahoma, Notre Dame, UCLA, Texas, and Penn State come to mind. Why shouldn't they? When was the last time you saw Bates and Bowdoin on national television? Yet, while it is true that Division I teams get the press, serious competition takes place at all levels, from Division I to the NAIA.

Although Division II teams do not contend at the same level as Division I, it provides intense competition for even the best high school athletes. Many Division II athletes were high school stars who wanted to play consistently for smaller schools.

66 *The only teams I ever watched during high school were the best in the country in their respective sports. Sure, it would be fun to play with the best, but, for me, playing is the most important thing. I never thought there would be such great competition and organization at a non-Division I school like Skidmore."*

—Matt Galvin, Skidmore College

Division III is different from Division I, Division II, and the NAIA in that it does not allow schools to provide athletic scholarships. Surprisingly, the level of competition, although somewhat less intense, remains high.

66 *I was surprised to find competitive swimmers at the Division III level. But what surprised me the most was the degree of seriousness that existed at a small, liberal-arts school in everything from the scheduling to the coaching."*

—Shelley Farmer, Vassar College

Less well known than the NCAA, the NAIA has adopted different recruiting policies, eligibility requirements, and scholarship strategies. In terms of competition, the NAIA sits on the same level as Division II or Division III in the NCAA ranks.

66 *I thought that NAIA schools were not competitive enough to be in the NCAA. I was dead wrong. They are quite competitive on the field and extremely serious about practice time."*

—Keith Vernon, University of Puget Sound

MYTH #3: COLLEGE ATHLETICS HINDER ACADEMICS.

Headline: Basketball Star Joe Dokes Can't Read; Sues Former School

Heard the story? Although these situations exist, they represent an exception to the rule. The majority of college athletes do not see athletics as detracting in any serious way from their academic pursuits. In fact, after questioning numerous college athletes, the consensus was that most received their *best* grades during the semester of their sport. Why? The athletes felt that having a sport to play forced them to balance their time and study more effectively.

66 *Competing in a varsity sport added some needed discipline to my day. If I was not out hitting the tennis ball, I would have just played around and wasted time anyway."*

—Geoff Tabin, former tennis team captain, Yale University

Still, the majority of student-athletes feel that it is best to take a "lighter load" during the season in which they play a sport. Why overburden yourself with academic units when you already have a huge athletic commitment?

Go For It, But Watch The Elbows!

❝ *Show me a good loser and I'll show you a loser."*

—Leo Durocher

Sure, everyone wants to win, but when playing club and intramural sports, remember that the same guys you elbow under the hoop are going to be sitting next to you in calculus class. So, take it easy unless you plan on studying differential integrals all by your lonesome.

In summary, go ahead and hit the three-pointers, but be careful with those elbows.

What If Organized Athletics Aren't For You?

There are plenty of ways to stay active while you are at college if you decide not to be part of an organized team.

First, check out your school's recreation center facilities. Most schools will have a pool, gymnasium, and weight/exercise facility that students have free access to with a student ID. So go swim a few laps before class, or pick up a game of two-on-two basketball before dinner, or if you're into the Stairmaster and treadmill, check out your school's equipment in that department.

You can also stay fit by taking up jogging, inline skating, or biking. These activities have the added bonus of getting you outside for some fresh air. Also, any one of these activities is a great way to explore the campus and surrounding area.

❝ *The day that I arrived home from school after freshman year I saw my high school principal in the airport. He said to me, 'Well, at least I can tell that they've been feeding you well!'*

When I got back to school I realized that I had become pretty sedentary and decided to start jogging every day. Not only did the jogging keep me in shape, but every day I tried to change my route a little bit, either by going down a new side street, heading off in another direction, or even just doing a route in reverse. It was a great way to explore town. I found myself jogging through beautiful neighborhoods lined with old colonial mansions that I didn't even know existed the year before. I discovered new restaurants and parks—it was really a great way to see the town."

—Daniel Baer, Harvard University

If you do take up jogging or the like, it's a good idea to find a buddy who wants to join you. Not only does jogging with a friend make it safer, but also it is much easier to discipline yourself to go if you know that someone else will be waiting for you!

But What About What Mr. Hutchins Said?

❝ *When I feel a desire to exercise, I lie down till it goes away."*

—Robert M. Hutchins (1935)

Ah, Bob was a wimp.

CHAPTER 18

Dating

" *All fall quarter I was dying to go on a date. Besides Nietzsche, that's practically all I thought about. The only problem was, I was too afraid to ask any woman out.*

I was terrified of rejection. What if she said no? What if she told all her friends what a nerd I was? And then they told their friends and so on and so on and so on. Pretty soon, the whole school would know.

So, instead of asking anyone out, I sat around thinking about Nietzsche some more. I hate Nietzsche. Meanwhile, my roommate was telling me I was a candidate for Dr. Ruth.

Finally, I did it. I asked out a girl in my economics class. She said yes. She didn't think I was a nerd. She didn't tell any of her friends. We went out for pizza and a movie.

And, you know something, I had a great time. Asking her out wasn't such a big deal after all."

—Greg Gottesman, Stanford University

Dating: The Anxiety Factor

Without a doubt, this is the most anxiety-provoking chapter in *College Survival*. Regardless of whether you are new to the scene or an old pro, dating brings illusions of pride lost, time wasted, and hearts broken. No one, no matter how attractive, is completely comfortable with the idea.

But the truth is, learning how to deal with members of the opposite sex is one of the most important skills you will learn at college. You should date, you will date, and you'll have fun doing it!

Following are some answers to the most commonly asked questions about dating at college. Later in the chapter, you will learn some helpful tips for your next date.

Some Common Dating Questions

1. WHAT ARE SOME EASY WAYS TO BREAK INTO THE DATING SCENE?

You will arrive at college without any of the titles or labels you bore in high school. Your old group of friends will have dispersed across the country. Now what do you do?

For starters, talk to people. Talk to anyone and everyone, in your dorm, Greek house, or wherever. Visit some of the people you met in your classes. Besides being the best way to make friends, this is also an excellent way to meet potential dates.

In terms of an actual one-on-one date, fraternity and sorority formals and even dormitory dances will provide you with a golden opportunity to ask someone out.

Remember, you don't have to know a person that well to go on a date with him or her. It's freshman year. No one knows anyone that well.

2. WHICH IS BETTER: THE GROUP DATE OR THE INDIVIDUAL DATE?

To ease the anxiety of an initial date, many freshmen opt for a group date. When you are double-dating (or have joined up with a group of friends with no one in particular as your date), interaction becomes much less intimidating. In fact, at many schools, group dating has become the preferred mode.

❝ *For me, group dating is much easier, particularly when you're first getting to know someone. When there are other people to talk to, it's easier to relax and to have a good time.*

When you're on your first date, it's hard enough to find something to talk about—especially for 5 hours.

You'll have plenty of time to get to know someone—if he's really someone you want to get to know. In the meantime, group dating is usually a more fun and a more relaxed way to meet someone."

—Kristen Whyte, University of Washington

What group dates provide in liveliness and comfort, however, they often lack in intimacy. If you excel at one-on-one interaction or if you really want to get to know someone, the group thing might cramp your style.

Many students start out by group dating and, once they get to know someone well, ask that person out on an individual date.

3. WHAT ABOUT THE GIRLFRIEND OR BOYFRIEND YOU LEFT AT HOME?

Many freshmen come to school missing an extra piece of baggage, mainly in the form of a boyfriend or girlfriend at home. Sometimes these long-distance relationships are able to weather the pressures of maturity and huge telephone bills, but, more often than not, they fail.

It is usually a good policy to date other people at college. If you are calling your long-distance sweetheart every day, chances are you will miss out on many new experiences and some invaluable opportunities for growth.

If you find yourself dreading the thought of making that call to your high school sweetheart to tell him or her that you've decided that the long distance thing just won't work, rest assured that you are not unique. All over the country there are freshmen in college who are making the same phone call. It isn't easy to do, but in the long run you both will probably be grateful for the decision.

    ❝ *During my freshman year at Pomona, I was still going out with my girlfriend from high school. She was going to college two hours away, and we spent a lot of time commuting back and forth.*

While at that time that was the only decision I could make, I later realized that I had missed out on making a lot of new relationships and in getting involved on my campus.

When your heart and mind are at another place, you pass up on many of the experiences of freshman year."

—David Muscatel, Pomona College

Even if you plan on being loyal to your boyfriend or girlfriend at home, figure out some way to have an active social life. In this case, finding a group of close friends may be your best bet.

Finally, don't become paranoid about losing your hometown boyfriend or girlfriend. If it's meant to be, you have nothing to worry about.

4. WHAT ABOUT SEX?

Some freshmen drown themselves in their newfound freedom. Out of the clutches of mom and dad, they feel like college is a time to experiment, a time to let it all hang out.

Whether or not you have sex at college is completely up to you. But don't get too carried away with your own freedom. When it comes to sex, be careful and be choosy. Just because people around you are doing it—and there will be plenty, perhaps even your roommate—doesn't necessarily mean you have to.

Four Tips on Successful Dating

There's nothing worse than a bad date. And you'll know when it's happening. Minutes will seem like hours, hours like days. Your stomach will turn. You'll start getting paranoid and anxious.

Ah, but never fear, *College Survival* to the rescue! While these next few tips cannot guarantee physical attraction, they should make your next date a little more interesting and definitely more enjoyable.

1. GO FOR IT!

One of the saddest realities about college is that students talk about dating more than they actually do it. People get caught up in the what-if-she-says-no or the what-if-he-doesn't-like-me game.

What students forget is that their classmates want to go out just as much as they do. Everyone wants to meet new people. Dating, although embarrassing at times, is a great way to do just that.

The problem with the next four tips is that, if you don't follow this first suggestion, the rest are moot. And, yes, it does take guts to ask someone out. But as Sir William Schwenck Gilbert once said, "Nothing ventured, nothing gained." Take a chance.

2. BE FUN AND CREATIVE.

When planning your dates, try to be creative. Dinner at your campus cafeteria may be practical, but it's certainly not going to win over any hearts.

Be a little different, if you can. Here are a few sure-fire suggestions:

Date Suggestions:

1. Picnic . . . romantic, practical, perfect
2. Local comedy show . . . laughs galore, great icebreaker
3. Major sporting event . . . expensive but fun
4. Hiking . . . romantic but sweaty
5. Bicycling to a restaurant . . . athletic, fun, romantic

If the creative juices just aren't flowing, don't fret. The pizza-movie date is always a great alternative.

 Psst . . . A lot of students like to stay on campus for their first date. It's practical and casual. Besides, most freshmen don't have cars, and campuses are loaded with things to do. Concerts, lectures, movies, plays, sporting events, pizza parlors, coffee shops . . . many a relationship has been started over a cup of cappuccino.

3. LISTEN.

One of the strange paradoxes of life is that people love talking about themselves, but very few people love listening to people who talk about themselves.

Instead of talking about yourself, ask your date lots of questions. The way to a person's heart is to have him or her know you care.

If you like the person, you'll have plenty of time to shine and to wax philosophically. In the meantime, listen up. Your date will think you're one in a million, which you will be.

66 *I had a friend who was dying to go out with this guy. He was handsome and seemed like he had a great personality. When he finally asked her out, she was practically counting down the days until the date.*

But the date itself was a complete disaster. The handsome guy turned out to be the most self-inflated, self-important, self-loving human being on the planet. All he talked about was himself—in the car, at dinner, everywhere. My friend barely even got a word in. To say that she couldn't stand this guy is an understatement.

By the end of the night, she was sick—literally. She wanted to leave the date so badly that she started dry-heaving. It was the saddest thing I'd ever seen.

All I can say is that if you think talking about yourself is going to impress someone, think again. Listening works better."

—Leslie Friend, University of Chicago

4. WATCH OUT FOR SCAMMERS.

By the time most freshman women reach their sophomore year, they've heard as many pick-up lines as Kim Basinger. College is home to many a scammer.

But, in all seriousness, beware of guys who are more physical than you would like, or who try to entice you to do things you don't want to do.

Date rape is an ominous reality on most college campuses. Always use good common sense and be careful. If you are feeling uncomfortable, don't be afraid to leave. At the very least, state your intentions clearly.

Chapter 22, Campus Safety, covers this topic more extensively.

66 *My mother always told me: Beware of guys with wandering eyes. But the truth is, you have to beware of more than that. Guys that ask you to go up and look at their fish tank . . . . definite no-no. Guys that claim that they're related to someone famous . . . maybe, probably not. Guys that want to go for a walk but actually want to trek through the forest . . . later. Guys that emanate an odor that can be detected for a 10-mile radius . . . think again.*

Seriously, be picky. There are lots of great guys at college but there are also lots of iffy ones."

—Kim Benaroya, UC Santa Barbara

CHAPTER 19

Partying and Alcohol

66 *My friends and I had set out on a quest: to seek and consume as much alcohol as humanly possible. With my girlfriend at my side, I had an added incentive. I wanted to prove to her that I could drink like the god I was (or thought I was).*

The first four beers were easy. They went down cold and smooth. But, two beers later, I realized that my balance was shot. Besides that, all the women looked attractive, even the ones who weren't so great an hour ago. Beer goggles, yes!

Undaunted, I plowed through four more beers. I didn't even taste them. Then I danced and stumbled my way through an additional two and left the party at 1 A.M. By now, I was drunk. I had all the signs: blurred vision, slurred speech and a complete lack of balance. But, hey, I was a drinking deity! Right?

I returned to my friend's room only to find a bottle of vodka being passed around. After two shots, my personal time-space continuum went bad. The next thing I know, I am kissing this woman (not my girlfriend) and, a little later, throwing up in the toilet.

Yes, I had become a fallen god. I was sick.

And to make matters worse, my roommate's parents showed up at the door at 9 A.M. the next morning.

What did I learn? I learned that drinking twelve beers and then doing vodka shots is akin to hitting yourself over the head with a baseball bat. I learned that the actual act of getting sick is nothing any god would want to play any part in. And I learned that everyone has a limit as to how much they can drink. On that night, I surpassed mine."

—Bryan Cohen, Claremont McKenna College

Partying and Alcohol: The Realities of College

Partying at college is kind of like The Blob. You can't escape it. It will be a part of your life, regardless of where you go to school.

But while parties are part of the social scene at every college, the types of parties will differ with each school. At smaller, private schools, for example, the party scene may consist of gatherings of around 20 or 30 people, with alcohol and rowdiness at a minimum. At large "party" schools like Chico State or Arizona State, however, you may find scenes befitting the movie *Animal House*. Every day.

One thing will be the same at every party at every school: alcohol. Regardless of whether your campus is dry (alcohol is not allowed) or wet, you will have to make some tough decisions concerning alcohol consumption.

While *College Survival* does not condone or condemn drinking, it realizes that alcohol will play some role in your college life. Following are five tips to help you deal with two of college's biggest realities: partying and alcohol.

 Psst . . . Some of you probably are wondering why other recreational drugs are not covered extensively in this or other chapters. The truth is, drugs are "out" on most college campuses. This is not to say that people don't use them, but that alcohol is the drug of choice at this time. Still, all of these tips can be applied to other drugs.

Five Partying and Alcohol Tips

1. DON'T DRINK AND DRIVE.

Eloquence isn't needed here: Drinking and driving is just plain dumb. Besides, there's no excuse for it. Many alternatives exist. For example, many students have started assigning a "designated driver," a person who does not drink and is responsible for transportation to and from a party with alcohol.

❝ *I met Neil, Adam, and James the first day I arrived at Georgetown. We became friends and started trekking to all the big parties to drink and experience the joys of freshman year.*

Three weeks into school, we climbed into Neil's old Ford Thunderbird and took off with a half gallon of rum and a case of beer to crash a party at the yacht club on the Potomac. After many hours of drinking from a fully stocked bar, I headed back to the car. With a very drunk Neil at the wheel, we somehow made it back to the university parking lot, only then to wreck four cars while trying to pull into a parking space at 30 miles per hour.

Neil was arrested. Adam, James, and I were just warned by the Adjudication Board, and the incident was recorded on our disciplinary record. After that, I stayed away from my new friends. When I look back upon it, I see an insecure freshman who desperately needed friends and who almost risked his life because of it. Now I have many close friends at college . . . Neil, James, and Adam are not among them."

—Matt Carr, Georgetown University

College campuses are into the act as well, offering "safe-ride" programs. This service, which is usually free, allows students to call at any time from any place to receive a "safe" ride home.

Taxis and buses are other options. Besides that, you can always spend the night at the party's locale. Classmates usually don't mind you crashing on their couch or floor, especially if you're too drunk to drive.

2. KNOW YOUR LIMIT.

❝ *I was at a punk rock theme party and, believe me, I was playing the part. Chains surrounded my body. Handcuffs dangled from my small black mini-skirt.*

Before long, I found my way to the upside-down margarita room and positioned myself for maximum consumption. In the next hour, I must have drunk around ten upside-down margaritas. Feeling social and unaware of the nature of tequila, I then poured down a truckload of tequila poppers. Soon enough, the alcohol hit, and I found myself hugging the cool porcelain.

I awoke the next morning at 5 A.M. surrounded by chains and handcuffs. I decided to make the trek back to my room and, if things hadn't been bad enough, the wind outside resembled a typhoon somewhere in the Philippines.

So, here I was . . . freezing, hung over, and swearing that the next time I would know my limit."

—Tina Santos, University of Puget Sound

Whether it's peer pressure or just plain thirst, it's very likely you will try drinking alcohol at college. If you drink too much, count on getting sick. Really sick. Although people have different tolerance levels, four beers or the equivalent in hard liquor is usually enough to cause damage—to your brain cells, if nothing else.

 Psst . . . Here's an equation you might want to commit to memory: 1 beer = 1 glass of wine = 1 shot of hard liquor.

3. DON'T WEAR NICE CLOTHES.

❝ *I had just gotten a new brown suede jacket and wanted to wear it to the big party that night. But about half way through the evening, some guy spilled jungle punch all over my jacket. It took a trip to the dry cleaners and a few twenties to get the stain out.*

Next time I'll leave the new stuff at home and party in the stuff I don't care so much about."

—Jill Tacher, UC Santa Barbara

Here's a little *College Survival* addendum to Murphy's Law: The chance of someone's spilling a drink on you is directly proportional to the cost of the clothes you are wearing.

Nice clothes and shoes are magnets for any item that stains permanently. This doesn't mean you should dress like a slob when going to a party, but avoid wearing your best duds.

Remember that alcohol affects balance.

4. DON'T BELIEVE EVERYTHING YOU HEAR.

Liquor before beer/have no fear.

Beer before liquor/never been sicker.

—Unknown

Ah, the infamous college saying. But according to most doctors, this oft-repeated adage holds little truth.

What matters is how much you drink, not what type or in what order. Don't drink ten shots of hard liquor before having a few beers just because you heard it won't make you sick. It will.

5. FIND A BALANCE BETWEEN PARTYING AND ACADEMICS.

66 *I took chemistry in college, expecting the same results I got in high school. The only problem is, I partied until the night before the first midterm and bombed the test. Needless to say, my grade was closer to the right end of the alphabet than the left.*

After that, I realized that partying at college is fine, but you have to keep it in perspective. I set some limits for myself, and my transcript thanked me for it from then on."

—Betty Baugh Harrison, University of North Carolina

Finding a balance between socializing and academics is integral to college success. Too much partying and you may find yourself on academic probation.

Don't let the brainiacs who get straight A's and party five nights a week fool you. Besides, your tuition check is supposed to go toward an education, not Miller Lite.

To paraphrase Aristotle, quite a wine drinker himself: "Virtue comes from following a course of action somewhere between the extreme of too much and that of too little."

CHAPTER 20

Get Ready to Be Sick: Medical, Dental, and Psychological Care

66 *During winter quarter, I was plagued by a nagging cold. Even though I felt lousy, I didn't want to cut down on my activity load. I had just joined a fraternity, was involved in intramurals, and wanted to keep up my grades, not to mention getting to know that girl in my economics class a little better.*

When the cold didn't go away and I started running a high fever, I realized I needed to take it easy.

Two weeks later, I ended up at home, missing two weeks of school with mononucleosis.

Next time, I won't play doctor . . . I'll go to one."

—David Muscatel, Pomona College

Preventive Medicine

Everyone should practice preventive medicine; indeed, the best cure for ailments is not getting them in the first place. At the very least, heed these three pieces of advice:

1. Get adequate sleep

2. Maintain a well-balanced diet

3. Stay away from others who are sick

Obviously, circumstances such as finals and weekend parties will prevent perfect observance of these three commandments. But follow them whenever possible.

Where Should You Look for More Information?

Be careful [when] reading health books.
You may die of a misprint.

—Mark Twain

Symptoms and treatments for upper respiratory illnesses, gastrointestinal problems, sexually transmitted diseases, and other common ailments are mentioned in the following sections. For more information on these illnesses, consult *The Campus Health Guide* by Carol L. Otis, M.D., and Roger Goldingay.

Upper Respiratory Infections

BRONCHITIS AND PNEUMONIA

If you have been coughing severely for five or six days, and have chest pain and/or shortness of breath, you may have bronchitis, an infection of the respiratory tubes. Even worse, you could have pneumonia, an infection of the lungs. Go to the doctor immediately.

THE COMMON COLD

Infamous signals of the common cold include a runny nose, sneezing, watery eyes, and sinus congestion. While antihistamines can help the sinuses and Tylenol the aches and pains, nothing works better than pumping fluids and taking in some extra shut-eye.

Psst . . . Most cold medicines contain antihistamines, which can cause drowsiness—not so great if you have a midterm in the morning! Cough suppressants also can make you drowsy, as they may contain significant amounts of alcohol (Nyquil is 50 proof!). Ask the pharmacist for medicines that will not make you fall asleep (such as Sudafed for the sinuses and a runny nose and Robitussin for the cough).

THE FLU

Do you have chills? What about aches, pains, and a high fever? Watch out! You may have the flu.

Acetaminophen (for example, Tylenol) will be most effective against the fever, chills, aches, and headaches, while an over-the-counter cough suppressant can lessen a harsh cough.

As with colds, however, rest and fluids will work better than any drug.

Doctors suggest not taking aspirin to relieve flu and cold symptoms because of its recent connection with Reye's syndrome. Reye's syndrome involves liver and kidney failure and has been linked to aspirin—when used to combat viral illnesses.

MONONUCLEOSIS

The infamous "kissing disease," which can be spread through direct contact, starts with chills, a fever, a sore throat, and swollen glands.

The most conspicuous signal, however, is fatigue. If you feel unusually tired for a more than a few days, you may have mononucleosis. Do not pass "Go." Do not collect $200. See a doctor immediately.

STREP THROAT

This treatable bacterial infection is characterized by a nasty sore throat and fever. Caused by the *Streptococcus* bacteria, strep throat may be indistinguishable from a common viral sore throat. Untreated, strep can lead to complications, including rheumatic fever and kidney problems. See a doctor for a throat culture if your symptoms persist longer than two days.

Gastrointestinal Problems

HEPATITIS

Symptoms of this serious disease include weakness, loss of appetite, nausea, vomiting, dark-brown urine, and jaundice—a yellowish discoloration of the skin and tissues.

If you think you have hepatitis, seek medical attention immediately.

STOMACHACHES AND DIARRHEA

Most students choose greasy fast foods over balanced meals. This type of chaotic diet leads to stomach problems. Products like Kaopectate™ and Imodium A-D™ help diarrhea, while Tums™ and Rolaids™ can relieve an upset stomach. But don't fool yourself. Eating sensibly works best.

 Psst . . . Don't take aspirin for a stomachache. It can be a stomach irritant!

Sexually Transmitted Diseases (STDs)

Most students have an "I'll never get it" attitude about sexually transmitted diseases (STDs). Don't ask for trouble. Take preventive measures like using a condom.

If you have had intercourse with a person who is found or is suspected to have an STD, see a physician or go to an STD clinic immediately. The embarrassment is worth avoiding later complications.

Many campus health centers now have an anonymous testing service that is available to students. So, even if you are just a bit concerned, it is worth it to have peace of mind. Go get tested.

If you have an STD, you should tell your partner(s) so that he or she may be checked as well. Even though it may be difficult to confront your partner, he or she deserves to avoid any unnecessary complications due to your delay.

 Psst . . . If you are sexually active, make sure contraceptive devices are easily accessible. Don't assume your partner has taken the necessary precautions. And, remember, oral contraceptives do not protect against STDs.

AIDS

The most recent studies suggest that three in every 1,000 college students have the AIDS virus; but, according to many reports, the figure is even higher. This disease is predominantly transmitted through intercourse or the sharing of contaminated needles. AIDS kills. There is no cure at this time.

Be careful. Wear a condom. Don't share needles. Your life may depend on it.

CHLAMYDIA

Chlamydia, an infection in the vagina or urethra, is characterized by burning and frequency of urination. A bacterial STD, chlamydia is treatable with antibiotics. See a physician. Your partner, even if he or she is showing no signs of the disease, should be treated simultaneously.

GONORRHEA

Gonorrhea, caused by a bacteria called *Neisseria gonorrhoeae*, is characterized in men by painful discharge or burning during urination. In women, no symptoms usually occur until the Fallopian tubes and ovaries are infected. This leads to what is commonly called pelvic inflammatory disease or PID. Severe abdominal pain, a fever, and chills are hallmarks of PID. If you think you may have contracted gonorrhea, see a doctor immediately.

HERPES

Herpes, a viral STD, produces blisters on the penis or labia and the mucous membranes. The moderately painful sores caused by herpes viruses usually dry up and disappear in about two weeks. Once contracted, herpes cannot be cured, and the herpes virus may keep reactivating. If you think you might have contracted herpes, seek medical attention. Some antiviral prescription medications may alleviate the severity of an outbreak.

SYPHILIS

This now-rare venereal disease begins with the formation of a relatively painless sore or ulceration in the genital region. If you see sores in these areas of your body, seek medical help as soon as possible. Once the sores go away, you still may have the disease, but the diagnosis will be much harder to make.

WARTS

Warts or condylomata, infections caused by the papilloma virus, start as small flesh-colored growths. They are usually painless but will multiply throughout the genital region if not treated. Condylomata are associated with cancer of the cervix in women. If you see those infections, see a physician immediately.

Miscellaneous Ailments

It's no longer a question of staying healthy.
It's a question of finding a sickness you like.

—Jackie Mason

ACNE

Welcome to Acne, Part II: The College Years. Contrary to popular belief, food and drinks like chocolate, nuts, root beer, and Coca-Cola do not directly cause acne. Nevertheless, they may increase the severity of an outbreak.

Over-the-counter products that contain benzoyl peroxide, sulfur, resorcinol, and salicylic acid work well. Still, no better prevention exists than gentle cleansing of your face on a daily basis.

If the problem is serious, a doctor may be able to provide further help with a prescription drug.

ATHLETE'S FOOT

If you wear socks made of nonbreathing material and if your feet are often wet, the "Foot" may be stomping on your door.

A contagious affliction, athlete's foot can be treated with Micatin™, Tinactin™, or Zeasorb-AF™. Preventive measures include wearing cotton or wool socks, changing them frequently; keeping your shoes dry; wearing thongs in community showers; and drying your feet after showering (maybe even using a blow dryer).

HANGOVERS

❝ *As far as my guaranteed hangover cure, it rests on the firm foundation of scientific fact. Alcohol is a poison. Your body does not like to have alcohol in it. It will do virtually anything it can to get it out. That includes peeing it out, diluted in a lot of water. This leads you to get very dehydrated, among other things. Very simply, alcohol dries you out. When we want to dry stuff out in my chem lab, we soak it in pure ethanol (think Everclear). A hangover is simply your body's reaction to spending a very long time (say, overnight) badly dehydrated. So, how should we avoid hangovers? By taking special pills? Toast and black coffee? Mysterious incantations? Summoning spectral monsters to do our bidding? No, silly, you drink water before you go to bed. And lots of it. I recommend at least three BIG cups of water after serious drinking. Yes, you will have to pee. But that was a sacrifice you were willing to make in the first place, right?"*

—David Sivak, Harvard University

Water. Water. Water. More water.

If you are going to drink alcohol at a party, try to alternate between alcoholic and nonalcoholic beverages (such as water). Drink a few glasses of water before going to bed as well.

If you wake up feeling dehydrated, you may counter it by drinking—what else?—water.

Time is the only sure cure for a hangover-in-progress, but Alka Seltzer™ may make the wait more bearable.

HEADACHES

Because of increased tension, headaches are prevalent in college. To cure them, some recommend tossing down analgesics such as aspirin, acetaminophen, or ibuprofen (for example, Advil). Take these pharmaceuticals at the onset of a headache, not after the pain has become intolerable.

When aspirin fails, Leslie Friend, a junior at the University of Chicago, suggests having someone massage your neck and scalp. "It works better than you think," Friend says.

For recurring or severe headaches, consult a physician.

SLEEPING PROBLEMS

❝ *My roommate never sleeps. I mean, the guy comes in at 5 A.M. every morning and gets up at 9 A.M. Four hours of sleep . . . can you believe it? But, the thing is, he never gets tired. To top it off, he gets mad at me for turning off the lights and going to sleep at 1 A.M. I go to sleep at a normal hour and get yelled at."*

—Rick Arney, Stanford University

Regardless of where you live in college, there will be some students who stay up until 4 A.M. talking about anything from the benefits of liquid soap to the astrophysics of mauve bowling balls. If you cannot stay up this late, don't get trapped by the David Letterman fans. Figure out a way to obtain your required amount of shut-eye. Of course, this varies from person to person. Most can get by with less than they think. Rumor has it Napoleon conquered Europe on just 3 hours of sleep a day. If you are constantly coming down with infections, however, you are probably one of those people who requires more. You can conquer Europe next year.

Eight to ten hours of sleep is recommended, especially prior to and during finals week.

 Psst . . . Be very careful with sleeping pills and other products that are designed to induce sleep. Taking sleeping pills is dangerous if done too often or if taken in more than the recommended dosage. Instead of sleeping pills, you might look into natural remedies such as melatonin or even a glass of warm milk!

SPRAINED ANKLES

Getting through college without spraining your ankle at least once is next to impossible.

If you twist or sprain an ankle, pack it in ice intermittently for 24 to 48 hours—don't apply heat! Bags of frozen peas make good ice packs and can be refrozen and used again.

Immobilize the sprained area with an Ace™ bandage and elevate it as soon as possible. An anti-inflammatory medication (such as Advil™ or Aleve™) may help cut down on the pain and swelling. You should see a doctor as soon as possible.

If the swelling or pain seems inordinate, you may have to take more drastic measures. Severe sprains and fractures can be indistinguishable from each other. Immobilize the area, ice it, and seek medical attention pronto.

What About Medical Insurance?

When you broke your arm in sixth grade, you probably were not aware of the cost or the paperwork involved.

Breaking your arm in college is a whole different story. Mom won't be there to hold your hand or to take care of the insurance papers. As Humphrey Bogart said, "You're on your own, kid."

At college, you should consider two medical insurance options:

1. FAMILY MEDICAL INSURANCE

Family medical insurance policies differ in eligibility requirements and coverage. You and your parents should find out if you are still covered under the family's plan. Blue Cross, for example, will provide coverage until a son or daughter turns 23 years old.

While some plans pay for all expenses, including prescriptions and hospitalization, other policies cover only major costs, such as operations. Before leaving home, understand what your family's plan includes.

2. SCHOOL MEDICAL INSURANCE PLANS

Most schools offer low-cost student medical insurance plans, covering a variety of services. Again, know what you are entitled to under each specific plan.

Basic medical coverage at the University of Washington runs under $800 a year; it is pretty standard around the country.

THE COLLEGE HEALTH SERVICE FEE: A NECESSARY EXPENDITURE

In addition to selecting an insurance policy, you may have to pay a health service fee at registration. For roughly $100, you receive medical consultation and psychological counseling. Some schools throw in over-the-counter drugs as well. Although the medical care is notoriously bad at campus health centers, it can come in handy if you sprain your ankle or need a professional diagnosis.

Dental Health Needs

Have a sharp pain in your mouth? Maybe you need a cavity filled? Thankfully, there is no shortage of dentists.

While many students take care of routine dental work at home, some students like to find a new dentist at college. Ask older students and your dorm adviser who they go to for dental care. Shop around.

 Psst . . . Daily brushing and flossing minimize dental maladies. Remember . . . the extra effort of good oral hygiene more than outweighs the pain and expense of a trip to the dentist's office.

Dental Payments

If you still see your hometown dentist exclusively, the cost will probably be taken care of just as it had been before you went to school. With a new dentist, however, you will have to work out a new payment system. Dental insurance is a good idea.

Following are some examples of typical dental costs in various states. Rates vary dramatically across the country. Expect to pay more in Chicago than in a small New England town.

Initial oral examination	$90
Teeth cleaning with routine checkup:	$75
Fillings:	$95–$130
Crowns:	$500–$800
Wisdom teeth extractions:	$155–$400

Dental Insurance

Dental insurance is independent of health insurance. Like health insurance, however, you may still be covered by your family's dental plan, or you may need to acquire your own.

Know how much of the bill your insurance covers. Will it pay for fillings, crowns, root canals, and teeth cleaning? Find out before taking the "fill."

Psychological Health Needs

College is a fantastic experience, and part of what makes it so great is that it is a very active, dynamic time in your life. There is so much going on—new academic endeavors, tons of new friends, discovering new things about yourself, and on and on. Sometimes all these different things get overwhelming—it happens to everyone, so don't worry if you start feeling overwhelmed yourself.

Although some cannot wait to leave home, others fear the inevitable good-bye. Homesickness affects almost everyone in some way. Many students feel the stress and strain of trying to maintain grades and have a social life at the same time. Others fall into and out of love for the first time. The whole first-year college experience can be quite overwhelming.

The one thing you have to remember is that bouts with depression are *normal;* there is nothing necessarily wrong with you. Most college students experience some "down time" at some point during their college career. You are not abnormal if you find yourself feeling depressed too. However, if you are constantly depressed or, worse yet, feeling suicidal, seek help. Many times students don't know where to go for help. Call your campus medical center and ask for the mental health department. Or, if it's urgent, just go to the emergency room; the staff will be happy to assist you.

Colleges offer counseling to help students, particularly freshmen, through the difficult first year.

Normally, you don't have to pay for this type of counseling. If you seek outside professional help, however, you will assume the cost.

 Psst . . . If you see a friend acting strange or particularly depressed, talk to him or her. Ask if he or she is feeling okay. A lot of times, the person is just looking for someone to talk to—someone who cares. If the person does not want to talk and seems suicidal, get professional help. Talk to your resident adviser or contact psychological services in the student health department.

A TYPICAL COLLEGIATE MENU:

BREAKFAST USUALLY CONSISTS OF HIGH-SUGAR-LOW-PROTIEN CEREALS.

FOR LUNCH A BURGER AND FRIES' ARE OBLIGATORY.

PIZZA AND BEER ARE STAPLES THAT CAN BE SERVED FOR DINNER AND BREAKFAST ALIKE....

Mmm

.... FINALLY, ALL OF THE ABOVE CAN BE COMBINED FOR A LIGHT MIDNIGHT SNACK...

OINK

CHAPTER 21

Nutrition: You Are What You Eat

66 *For the first few weeks of college, I was a madman when it came to the cafeteria. Mom never stocked cola in the fridge at home. Now I could drink it whenever I wanted. Mom never let us eat sugar cereals. Now I could eat Frosted Flakes every morning. Mom never let us skip a main course for two extra desserts. Now I could eat ice cream and Jell-O for the main course.*

But, after the first two weeks, I understood why mom never let me have a field day in the kitchen. It wasn't that I was getting fat, although I did put on a few pounds. Rather, I had no energy. I couldn't do my work as fast. I couldn't get to the same balls on the tennis court. I took more naps. Sure enough, I found out that "you are what you eat." Not enough nutritious foods and too much sugar wear you down.

These days I stay away from soda pop and the one or two extra desserts. I feel better, and I work better, too."

—Greg Gottesman, Stanford University

Nutrition Tips

Upon entering college, you are going to have more freedom than ever before: freedom to stay up all night, freedom to wear your hair any way you want, and freedom to eat more junk food than you ever imagined!

But there are consequences attached to this new freedom. If you don't eat correctly, you will pay the price in stomach cramps, fatigue, and a wardrobe of clothes one size too small.

As Ben Franklin said, "One should eat to live, not live to eat."

If you sign up for a full or partial meal plan at college, you will have the opportunity to eat healthfully—in your dorm cafeteria or in other food centers on campus. Most cafeterias offer a salad bar, fruit, several entrees, drinks, and a choice of desserts.

Here are six tips for balancing your meals as recommended by the United States Department of Health.

1. Eat a variety of foods from the four food groups: meat, grain, dairy, and fruit/vegetables.
2. Avoid too much fat, saturated fat, and cholesterol.
3. Eat foods with adequate starch and fiber.
4. Avoid too much sugar.
5. Avoid too much sodium (salt).
6. If you drink alcoholic beverages, do so in moderation.

Avoiding the Infamous "Freshman Fifteen"

Face it, Mom didn't let you eat pizza every night, ice cream whenever you wanted, and McDonald's french fries twice a day. She also didn't let you stay up and drink beer with your buddies until dawn. Without knowing it, college students find themselves consuming fatty foods and calorie-filled beverages at double the previous rate. Ten pounds. Fifteen pounds. Twenty pounds. The increments steadily increase while you wolf down another burger or guzzle another beer.

❝ *When I went to college, the dorm food was just as bad as it is to-day. So, after dinner every night, I would devour a pizza, fried chicken, a deli sandwich, or a malted—not to mention a double-scoop Carvel ice-cream cone.*

Needless to say, by cleverly eating six meals a day, I gained 15 pounds. It wasn't until an acquaintance referred to me as 'that hulky girl' that I realized what I was doing."

—Laurie Meredith Weinman, New York University

Sherry, a Seattle nutritionist, has provided eight tips to help you keep unwanted weight where it belongs—on other people.

1. If you want to reduce the number of calories in your diet, focus on reducing the amount of fat. By consuming less fat, your calorie intake naturally will be reduced.

2. Increase the amount of fiber in your diet. (Fresh fruits, beans, and legumes are your best bet.)

3. Exercise often.

4. Avoid eating less than 4 hours before bedtime.

5. Avoid "empty calories," most prevalent in alcohol.

6. Consume six to eight glasses of water daily. Water is useful in metabolizing fat and replacing fluid loss from activity.

7. Don't try to lose more than 2 pounds per week. Those who try to lose tons of weight all at once are sacrificing muscle and water weight instead of fat.

8. Eat small, frequent meals rather than large, less frequent ones. Large meals, consumed many hours apart, trigger a starvation response, in which the body stores food instead of using it.

 Psst . . . Dieting is not always as easy as a trip to the salad bar. In fact, a salad with two helpings of ranch, bleu cheese, or other creamy dressings may have just as many calories as a hot fudge sundae. Be careful!

❝ *Most students gain their first year of college. I lost.*

It wasn't easy. I tried to make dinner a social event rather than an eating event. The hardest things, though, were trying to deal with the late-night munchies and the parties. Alcohol and pizza can put on extra weight like crazy. So, when other people were eating pizza, I chose fruit. When other people were drinking alcohol, I drank water.

It can be done. It just takes hard work and determination."

—JoEllen Tapper, Occidental College

Eating Disorders: Anorexia and Bulimia

❝ *Almost every girl I know in college has had an eating disorder at one time or another. Girls with absolutely perfect bodies would come into the dining room and eat everything in sight. Sometimes they would eat really fast and not let anybody see them. You could tell something was wrong."*

—Lauren Pass, Grossmont Community College

Thousands of college students, particularly women, suffer from two severe eating disorders: *anorexia nervosa* and *bulimia.*

According to Jacquelin, a registered nurse specializing in eating disorders, the problem usually starts at age 11 or 12 and escalates once in college. Societal pressures and family problems are the two biggest factors leading to the onset of these diseases.

❝ *I know many women who, when they are stressed about their grades or their boyfriend, automatically blame their problems on their bodies. They turn to crash diets and exercise programs.*

Don't get me wrong. Concern about your appearance is natural, and exercise and nutrition are extremely important for your health, but too many people ruin their bodies and their lives in a never-ending pursuit of thinness."

—Jeannie Heltzel, Stanford University

ANOREXIA NERVOSA

Anorexia nervosa, a disease in which victims deliberately starve themselves, can permanently damage the body and, in some cases, lead to death.

Those with this disease feel they are overweight, even if they are not. Symptoms include a severe lack of appetite, low self-esteem, excessive exercise, anxiousness, and a need for isolation.

Lauren Pass, a former anorexic, explains some of the symptoms. "If I ate just once, I wouldn't eat for two weeks after that—at all. I would exercise all the time. Those were the two most obvious signs."

BULIMIA

Those inflicted with *bulimia* binge on large quantities of food and then cleanse their systems through vomiting or laxatives. Symptoms include laxative abuse, dizziness, weakness, and a tendency toward perfectionism.

 Psst . . . You will be doing the suspected bulimic or anorexic a favor by expressing your concerns to a dorm adviser or to the school health facility.

Secret Drugs: Caffeine and Alcohol

CAFFEINE: ARE YOU SURE YOU WANT A SECOND CUP?

Many college students pray to the caffeine god. And why not? When a term paper is staring you in the face at 2 A.M., religious symbols provide little solace. Caffeine, on the other hand, can provide pages five through seven.

Found in products such as coffee, cola, chocolate, No Doz™, and Vivarin™, caffeine is a stimulant that increases your respiration, heart rate, blood pressure, and the secretion of various hormones. Simply put, it keeps you awake.

Although not addictive, caffeine is habit-forming. Sudden absence from the drug after long use leads to a withdrawal reaction, the most common symptom being a headache.

The American Heart Association recommends that consumption of caffeine be limited to fewer than two cups of coffee or caffeine-containing beverages per day. Overdoses may cause insomnia, jitteriness, nervousness, and intestinal discomfort.

So, if you are going to use caffeine, do so in moderation.

ALCOHOL: A WHOLE BUNCH OF EMPTY CALORIES?

66 *At Colby, we have a game called 'Beer Die.' You sit at either end of a table and depending on how the die land, someone has to drink. I played it every night for a month straight.*

The only problem was, after that month, I had built up a serious paunch—a world-class beer belly. I tried to cut back on food but kept drinking. Wouldn't you know it? The paunch stayed. I didn't exactly look like a champion on the beach that summer."

—Chuck Martin, Colby College

Most people know alcohol kills brain cells and is addictive; it is equally sinister from a nutritional standpoint.

Alcohol fills the body with "empty calories," calories without vitamins, minerals, or protein. These also are referred to as FAT calories. Indeed, the reason many students gain weight in college has nothing to do with increased food intake but, rather, increased alcohol consumption.

So, if you are planning on boozing it up night after night, don't be surprised when the "freshman fifteen" come knocking on your door.

CHAPTER 22

Campus Safety

66 *As at a lot of schools around the country, campus safety has become a big issue at Duke, particularly for women. The campus is really spread out, so the security people stress walking in groups and keeping to well lit areas at night. They also have escort services and give all the freshmen whistles in case of an emergency.*

I think all that stuff is great. But, let's face it, nothing beats good common sense. The best way to avoid bad situations is to not get into them in the first place. I always try to be aware of where I am and who I am with. I don't walk in 'questionable' areas alone. I don't put myself in situations where bad things are likely to happen."

—Heidi Wiedemann, Duke University

Be Aware and Alert!

Here are ten safety tips for college campuses. The first five concern protecting yourself outdoors and the next five inside your dormitory or Greek house.

Remember that these tips are not intended to make you paranoid. Just the opposite, in fact. They should make you feel like you have some control over your own safety, which you do, of course.

If you forget some of these tips, don't worry. Just remember the general idea that they all uphold: Use good common sense—which is the grand finale tip. This means always being alert and being aware of your surroundings.

1. STICK WITH GROUPS, ESPECIALLY AT NIGHT.

❝ *A lot of the women at Harvard ask us to walk them to the science center at night. It's a pretty long walk, but none of the guys mind. The women are never embarrassed to ask us, and we always do it. We just see it as a small way we can make our classmates feel a little more safe."*

—Robert Lloyd, Harvard University

Whether you're coming back from the library or returning home after a party, avoid walking alone. Sometimes it's easy to forget the simple truth: there is safety in numbers.

Don't feel embarrassed about asking a friend to walk you back to your room, preferably a male if you are a female. He or she probably will be flattered anyway.

And don't be afraid to use the campus escort services or safe rides. Most of the time the escorts are just waiting to be called upon. Use them; that's what they're there for.

2. DON'T JOG ALONE, ESPECIALLY AT NIGHT.

This tip seems pretty similar to the last one. Want to know why? Because it is . . . seriously, it cannot be repeated enough. Even students who are careful to walk in groups at night seem to forget this precaution when going out for a midnight or early-morning jog. Especially if you are a female, try to bring a companion.

3. WALK BRISKLY AND WITH PURPOSE.

❝ *My friends often make fun of me because I walk so fast. And sometimes they'll be following me for blocks before we realize that we have no idea where we're headed. This is because I never dawdle or walk as if I don't know exactly where I'm going. Granted, there are times when whizzing past everyone prevents me from smelling the roses. But, as my New York background has taught me, it's always better to be safe than sorry."*

—Noeleen Walder, Stanford University

It is always a good idea to look like you know where you're going, especially when walking alone. This means moving quickly and with some sort of purpose. Stopping a lot and talking to strangers often leads to trouble. Of course, this doesn't mean you should be suspicious of everyone who asks you a question. But use your intuition when strangers approach.

Also, don't be afraid to be rude. Your safety is much more important than the impression you give a stranger.

4. STAY IN WELL-LIT, POPULATED AREAS.

In general, it is a good idea to avoid dark areas. Don't take shortcuts unless you know they are well traveled and well lit. Campus police departments often prepare maps of suggested travel routes. If you have any doubts about which are the safest routes, use the maps.

5. DON'T FLASH VALUABLES.

Don't wear your fancy jewelry around the campus every day. Flashy items attract attention and make you an easy target.

You'll have plenty of opportunities to show off your best duds and jewelry at semiformals and so forth. In the meantime, leave the diamonds and the gold hidden in your room.

Also, remember to keep your purse zipped. It is easy to lose valuables when you set down a floppy handbag, and you don't want people eyeing your wallet.

 Psst . . . When you are moving through large crowds from class to class, it is better to keep your purse over your shoulder rather than clutched in your hand. Thieves will have a harder time grabbing something over your shoulder as opposed to snatching a bag out of your hand.

6. KEEP A LIST OF EMERGENCY NUMBERS HANDY.

You never know when you are going to have to call for help. And given the state of most college rooms, it is doubtful you will be able to find the telephone book at a moment's notice. So, keep a list of important numbers near the phone. You can even tape the list to the phone itself.

If you are in trouble and cannot figure out who to call, dial 911 . . . that's usually your best bet.

7. LOCK YOUR DOORS.

College campuses are notorious for theft. This doesn't mean you have to be suspicious of your next-door neighbor. Thieves from the local area know that college students tend to be apathetic about locking their doors, and they take advantage of it. So, take your keys with you and lock your door—always!

66 *When I first got to school, I used to leave the door unlocked when I went to the shower. But about four weeks into the quarter, that policy changed in a hurry.*

It was about 4 P.M., and I had just taken a shower after a rough basketball game. As I walked back into my room with only a towel covering me, I nearly bumped into a rather large man. Nope, it wasn't my roommate. I wish. The stranger was about 6-feet-4 and, let me tell you, he obviously had been to the gym a few times.

In the meantime, he seemed to be depositing several of the items from my roommate's desk into his pockets. His back was turned, and I politely asked him, terrified of course, 'Excuse me, but what do you think you're doing in my room?'

I obviously surprised him. He spun around and said, 'Um, can you tell me where the basketball arena is?'

'Well, it's certainly not in here,' I said. 'It's about 5 miles down the road.'

He looked at me and ran out the door.

Needless to say, from that time on, my roommate and I locked our door whenever we were out of the room—even if we were just going to the shower."

—Alex Berzins, Stanford University

8. DON'T LET STRANGERS INTO THE DORMITORY.

One of the best ways to protect yourself and your classmates at college is to prevent problems before they hatch. Not letting strangers into your dorm is the simplest and most effective way to do just that.

The doors to most college dormitories are locked. So, when a stranger wants to get in, don't be afraid to ask him or her the reason for the visit. If the stranger is associated with the campus, he or she will be more than happy to state his or her intent. It's also a good idea to ask whether the stranger has a student ID. If he or she doesn't, then you can say, "I'm sorry, but I can't let anyone in without an ID." It's better to be a little rude (and safe!) than sorry.

Also, try not to prop the doors open at night. Sure, waiting for the pizza delivery man by the door can be a drag, especially at 1 A.M. But, if you leave the door open, you are just begging for trouble.

9. BE CAREFUL IN THE ELEVATORS.

Big dormitories at big schools usually have elevators, and these can be a major source of problems.

Avoid riding up or down in the elevator with strangers, especially if you are a woman. If someone makes you feel uneasy while riding, get off at the next floor. Your safety is definitely worth the extra wait.

In addition, if the door opens and you don't like the contents, act as if you forgot something, walk away, and take the next elevator.

10. STAY CALM AND USE COMMON SENSE.

These ten tips may be helpful, but they certainly cannot take the place of simple common sense. College life will present you with many new situations. You will be living in your own room. You will be able to set your own hours. You will be able to attend parties or other social gatherings almost every night. Obviously you are not going to lock yourself up in a room. But there are dangers of which you should be aware.

The best advice, once again, is to use good common sense. Stay calm. Be aware of the situation you are in at all times. And don't be afraid to leave a party if it is getting out of hand or to "embarrass" someone if you feel uncomfortable.

Date Rape: The Reality on College Campuses

Officials at the University of Southern California and the Los Angeles Police Department are investigating a student's report that she was raped in a fraternity house while on a date last September and subjected to a party of mostly undressed [fraternity] members.

The student said the rape took place . . . last September. But police said she did not file a formal complaint until April."

—The *New York Times,* June 24, 1990

Date rape has become one of the biggest issues facing American colleges today. Date rape is defined as forced, manipulated, or coerced sexual acts by a friend or acquaintance occurring in a date-like situation. Following are three scary truths about date rape on college campuses today.

FACT 1:

In a recent survey of over 6,000 students from over thirty-two colleges across the country, one out of every six female students reported being a victim of rape or attempted rape during the preceding year.

—A. Adams, *Sexual Assault On Campus,* 1988

FACT 2:

Eighty-five percent of rapes on college campuses are acquaintance rapes.

—R. Warshaw, *I Never Called It Rape*

FACT 3:

In a Kent State University study, one in 12 men admitted to having fulfilled the prevailing definition of rape or attempted rape, yet none of these men identified themselves as rapists.

—M. Koss, Ms. *Magazine Campus Project on Sexual Assault,* 1988

Tips to Help You Avoid Date Rape

BE AWARE OF THE EFFECT OF ALCOHOL AND DRUGS

Drinking, especially beyond your "limit," interferes with clear thinking and effective communication. *Against Her Will*, a cable television program on the Lifetime Network, asserted that 75 percent of the men and 55 percent of the women are intoxicated during date rape.

Learn your limit—both men and women. Don't get so drunk that you do things you will regret the next day.

 Psst . . . Having sexual intercourse with someone who is drunk or, more specifically, a person who is incapable of resisting, is considered rape in a court of law.

COMMUNICATE YOUR LIMITS CLEARLY

If someone starts to offend you or make you feel uncomfortable, tell this person firmly and immediately that he or she is doing something you don't like. Say no when you mean no. Say it loudly and clearly.

PAY ATTENTION TO WHAT IS HAPPENING AROUND YOU

Watch for nonverbal clues (for example, if someone is touching you more than you are comfortable with). Try not to put yourself in vulnerable situations.

If you feel uncomfortable, the best thing to do is to leave. A lot of times a person will not want to offend the other party by making an early exit. Baloney! Your personal safety should come first.

STICK WITH A GROUP OF FRIENDS

There is safety in numbers. If a friend has partied too hard, take that person home and make sure she is okay. Don't let a friend wander off with a person of the opposite sex if she is intoxicated. Ask your friends to do the same for you. The drug Rohypnol (commonly known as a "roofie") has been in the news a lot lately. Because it is odorless and tasteless when slipped into a person's drink, rapists often choose Rohypnol when attempting to drug someone. Rohypnol is ten times more potent than Valium and is the inebriating equivalent of a six-pack of beer. The drug makes a person feel very relaxed, confused, and uninhibited, and sleepy. Too much can cause a person to pass out or, in extreme cases, die. If you are concerned about this particular drug—and you should be—you should fix your own drink when you go to a party, never leave a drink unattended, and be careful to watch what you drink.

DON'T BLAME YOURSELF

If you are raped, a common reaction is to blame yourself. Don't do it! Nobody asks to be raped!

Seek emotional support and see a doctor immediately for treatment of injuries or a rape exam.

THINK ABOUT REPORTING THE INCIDENT

Ultimately, reporting a rape is your decision. But the police encourage it for several reasons. First, an immediate report will allow valuable evidence to be collected. This increases the chance of apprehension and a successful prosecution.

Second, you will be providing official documentation necessary for criminal prosecution or civil redress if you later choose to pursue this course of action.

Finally, many rapists are repeat offenders. You will be providing information on a person who could be responsible for other assaults, thereby protecting yourself as well as others.

CHAPTER 23

Banking at College

❝ *Before I went to college, I didn't realize how many things I spent money on . . . food, gas, pencils, paper, books, clothes, and that's just for starters.*

If you think you can make it at college with just a few hundred dollars of spending money, you're kidding yourself. Going to a formal can run well over a hundred bucks, and that's not including the corsage.

If you're going to college, you're definitely going to need some spending money. And you're definitely going to need a bank to store it in."

—Justin Kennedy, Wesleyan University

Look Out for Hidden Expenses!

Hidden expenses often take college students by surprise. Most expect just the tuition bill and fees for room and board, but the other expenditures like midnight pizzas and textbooks add up to well over a few Andrew Jacksons. In other words, you cannot just stuff a few $20 bills in your wallet before you leave home and expect to survive. You need a bank.

Choosing a Bank

When choosing a bank, keep two things in mind:

1. Find a bank that has ATMs (automatic teller machines) within walking distance of your room.

2. Consider all possible hidden costs of the bank in question.

❝ *When choosing a bank, the important thing is to know what you want. What I needed was the basic services for the cheapest possible price. Every single bank has fees, whether they tell you about them or not.*"

—Ann Wilensky, Columbia University

Although most banks offer similar services, fees fluctuate. If you are not careful, you could end up paying $150 a year in service fees.

Taking Money to College

If you are transferring money from a savings account at your hometown bank to one at school, request a cashier's or bank check for the amount you want to take. The cost for a cashier's check will be minimal, if anything at all.

Consider leaving your hometown account open, because you probably will want to use it when you come home for holidays and summer vacation.

When opening a new account at school, a cashier's check may take a few days to clear, especially if you go to school out of state. So make sure that you have a bit of extra cash or a credit card with you to tide you over until the money in your account is available.

Forget Western Union!

Don't send your money to college by wire transfer. A bank charges you to send the money out, and then the receiving bank charges you again.

The result is a loss of $15 to $20. Western Union is even worse, charging you between $18 and $75. The only advantage to this method is that it's speedy.

Banking at an In-State School

Those who have chosen a local university should have no trouble selecting a bank.

If an ATM of your hometown bank is located near the university, stick with it. You will be able to do almost all necessary transactions without having to transfer your account.

Selecting the Best Account for Your Needs

If you are changing banks and need to open a new account, decide which banks are most popular among the students and then visit each one yourself.

When you enter a potential bank, walk up to an official behind a desk—not a teller—and inform him or her that you are thinking of opening an account. The banker may load you with scads of pamphlets. Be careful! Obtain literature only on those services that concern you: savings, checking, ATMs, and credit cards.

Make sure to ask if the bank offers a special student package. These plans are definitely worth looking into as they usually offer free or reduced service charges on ATMs as well as other incentives.

Also inquire about ATM charges on your bank's machine *and* other banks' machines. You will be using the ATM a lot. Choose an account with minimal or no ATM charges.

Savings, Checking, and Money Market Accounts

Before deciding which account or combination of accounts you need, understand the three different types of accounts: checking, savings, and money market.

CHECKING ACCOUNTS

Because you will have some big bills to pay at college, you should get a checking account. Banks generally have three types of checking accounts: normal, limited, and interest-bearing.

The *normal option* requires a minimum balance of $300 to $500. If you stay above this balance, the bank charges no monthly fee. Falling below results in a penalty charge. The disadvantage of this option is that you earn no interest.

The *limited-option* checking account enforces no minimum balance and lets you write up to ten checks a month—more than enough for most college students. This account often costs about $1.75 a month. With the limited option, you can take the minimum balance you had in the normal option and put it into savings. This will earn a few bucks in interest throughout the year. Of course, with the limited option account, you pay about $20 a year in monthly checking fees. Before making a decision, realize that many banks offer special limited accounts to students in which no fee is charged for checks or for monthly use. This could be your best bet.

For those with a very nice nest egg, an *interest-bearing* checking account allows you to earn interest while keeping your money available for checking. In most cases, you can earn interest as long as your average monthly balance does not dip below a certain amount at any time. The charge when letting your account slip below the required minimum is rather steep. If you have the available funds and remain wary, an interest-bearing checking account may be your best option.

SAVINGS ACCOUNTS

Usually $100–$300 is enough to open a savings account. Regardless of the bank you choose, these accounts pay more interest than an average checking account (which usually pays no interest). There should be no charge for depositing or withdrawing money.

On the negative side, you cannot write checks with many savings accounts. Furthermore, if your account drops below the minimum assigned by the bank (such as $100), you will be charged a slight fee.

While some banks compound interest annually, others quarterly, and others daily, computer analysis shows it makes only a miniscule difference in earnings at year's end.

Because interest rates and interest earnings rarely vary, the three most important criteria for judging a savings account should be:

1. What is the minimum balance?
2. How much do I get charged if I dip beneath the minimum balance?
3. Is there any fee for using the ATM?

Many students opt for a savings account along with a checking account. They keep most of their money in their savings account, which earns higher interest, and transfer funds when their checking account dwindles.

MONEY MARKET ACCOUNTS

The money market account has several advantages:

1. It offers you a higher rate of interest than the normal checking account as long as you maintain a minimum balance.
2. It does not require a monthly service fee above the minimum balance.

The disadvantage is that often you are allowed only three checks per month, leaving just one for tuition, one for housing, and the last for the phone bill. If you do write an extra check or if your account slips below the minimum balance, the bank charges you a stiff fee. Also, most banks do not let you earn interest when you go below the minimum balance.

With some online bill paying software offered banks, you can draw money from any account. If you are paying your bills online, the number of checks you need becomes less important.

Depositing Money: Use the ATM!

Each time you receive money, whether it be a paycheck or that $20 bill Grandpa handed you beneath the dinner table, you should deposit it immediately into your bank account. By depositing your money as quickly as possible, you avoid losing it and start earning interest, depending on your account.

The easiest and fastest way to deposit funds is to use the ATM. Don't fear ATMs! They are extremely accurate and will never swallow up your money for no reason.

Go to the ATM machine, usually open 24 hours a day, and insert your card. The machine then will ask you for your access code.

 Psst . . . Never tell anyone about this code, not even your roommate. You can always find a better way to get some money. Don't let anybody use your card!

Once you enter your code, the machine will ask you what kind of transaction you want. In this case, you press "deposit." You will then be asked to input the amount. If you input the wrong number, simply press "cancel" and start over.

After you have typed in the amount, the machine will tell you to insert the envelope containing your check into a special compartment. Make sure you endorse the back of the check with your signature, along with the words "for deposit only" and your account number. With regard to your account number, you may have different ones for your various accounts: checking, savings, and/ or money market. Make sure you write down the correct one. Once the check has been deposited, the machine will issue you a receipt and you're on your way. Not so fast! Don't forget to take your card out of the machine and don't forget to record the transaction in your checkbook—whether it be a deposit or a withdrawal.

ATM Problems to Avoid

ATMs allow you to bank without ever actually entering one—a bank, that is. But, despite making banking a lot easier, ATMs bring some new problems to the world of finance. Here are three important don'ts for ATM users.

DON'T LOSE YOUR CARD

If you lose your ATM card, call the bank as soon as possible. Most banks have 24-hour numbers, which you should have on file both in your wallet and in your dorm room.

DON'T GO TO THE ATM ALONE AT NIGHT

Try to go to the ATMs during the day, especially if your bank is in the city. If you do have to use one at night, go with a friend.

DON'T ABUSE YOUR ATM PRIVILEGES

ATMs make it extremely easy to withdraw money. After pushing the "withdraw" button too many times, you may begin to think your ATM card is a product of the devil. But if you keep good records and remember to record your withdrawals and deposits, you shouldn't have any problems.

DON'T USE OTHER BANKS' ATMS IF POSSIBLE

If you use an ATM machine owned by another bank, expect to pay a $1.50–$2.00 service fee each time. Those charges add up over time. You should make going to your bank's ATM machine a part of your weekly or monthly routine so that you don't find yourself needing cash when you're in strange places. Also remember, your bank may charge you a fee of $5.00 or more each time you use an ATM machine outside of the U.S. Keep that in mind if you plan to head for Cancun for spring break!

Keeping Track of Your Checking Account

Many college students don't see the purpose behind recording checks and deposits. Doesn't the bank do it anyway? Hold the phone!

Not only do good records bar you from dipping below the minimum balance and being charged a fee, they also prevent you from overdrafting your account (having a negative balance).

Besides, banks make errors! At the end of a month, the bank will send a statement with all your banking transactions. This will include an outline of the amount withdrawn, the amount deposited, and the amount deducted in fees and charges. The balance you have at the bottom of your checkbook should match exactly the balance that the bank sends you, excluding any deposits and/or checks that have not cleared (see the formula that follows). If the two do not match and you have rechecked your figures carefully, call the bank.

If you don't want to do the addition and subtraction yourself, you can use a computer program like Quicken or Microsoft Money to keep track of your account activity. It will add or subtract all your entries for you and store your records. Remember to include your ATM withdrawals!

THE FORMULA

Your Balance = Bank's Balance – Uncleared Checks + Uncleared Deposits

 Psst . . . One of the best ways to keep adequate records is to order duplicate checks. This type of check has a carbon copy behind each original check. Everything you write on the original is reprinted on the carbon copy. Thus, if you forget to enter an amount, you can always go back and check the stack of duplicates.

You Are in Demand!

Selecting the "right" bank and the "right" combination of accounts can fluster even the most organized student. With so many banks to choose from and so many options to sift through, students often forget who is in the driver's seat.

You are!

Realizing that today's college graduates will be tomorrow's achievers, banks are vying for your business. They want to establish a financial relationship with you, hoping it will continue in the future.

If you remember who is in control, who the desired customer is, and whose business the banks want, selecting a bank becomes much less intimidating.

Credit Cards

These days money in college is all about the credit card. Credit cards are so widely accepted that you can buy almost anything with them—books, furniture, food, and basically all your essentials. Having a credit card in college is a great convenience for most students, but as with any convenience, it has its price. The following section lists several tips for minimizing trouble and maximizing convenience when it comes to credit cards.

1. APPLY FOR STUDENT CARDS.

Most of the major card companies (Visa, MasterCard, American Express, and Discover) now offer a special application for student card holders. Look for a card that has *no annual fee*. You don't want to get stuck paying a heap of money every year just to have your card.

Some credit cards come with added bonuses, such as frequent-flier airline miles for every dollar spent or a percentage kickback to a favorite charity or affinity group for every purchase. These added features are great, but you should still look at the entire deal. For example, a frequent-flier credit card may come with an annual fee and a higher interest rate than a student card, making choosing such a credit card more difficult. These special credit cards are usually best for students who know they will be paying their entire credit card bill on time all the time. You can call your favorite airline or affinity group to ask more about these credit cards.

2. PAY OFF YOUR CARD WHEN THE BILL COMES EVERY MONTH.

Credit card companies make their money in two ways. First, they charge stores a fee for each purchase made with a credit card. Second, they make money by charging interest to cardholders who do not pay on time. The interest charged on a credit card usually starts out with a "low introductory rate" but quickly climbs to an astronomical level, often as high as 18 percent annually or more.

In order to avoid falling prey to the card company, make a habit of paying off your credit card every month when the statement arrives. Don't put it off until next month so that you have extra cash for the weekend. That "extra cash" will be spent on interest and fees before you know it.

3. SHOP WITH CARE.

Just because you have a credit limit of $600 doesn't mean that you should spend that much! Be careful with your credit card, and remember that you should have money in your bank account to cover every purchase you make on your card. Keep track of how much you are spending on your card by saving your receipts in your wallet. When they start to pile up, slow down!

4. PROTECT YOUR CREDIT RATING.

The reason that it is so important to be careful with your credit card is that if you are always late on payments, or if you fail to pay off your card, the credit card company has the power to destroy your credit rating.

Your credit rating will be very important down the road when you want a loan to buy a new car or house. In fact, if you have a credit card and are responsible about paying off the balance, the card company will record that as well, and your credit rating will improve.

5. BE SMART.

Basically, a credit card requires responsibility. If you know that you are a big spender and that a credit card would send you out of control, then it might be best to stick to cash and checks. But for most students, a credit card can be a remarkably convenient addition to a wallet.

Psst . . . Depending on your arrangements with your parents about what they will pay for while you are at college (if anything at all), you may want to get two credit cards. One for you and one for expenses like books for which mom and dad have agreed to help.

Last but Not Least: A Word on Budgeting

" *It is difficult to learn the meaning of fiscal responsibility, especially when you've got a new Visa card and there's a great-looking sweater in the shop window. It's even harder when the sweater is on sale.*

My mom told me not to go over $200 on my card. I had finals to take and, as my apartment was off campus, I rented a car for finals week, hoping to use my free time for study. During the month, I had charged a few sweaters and a pair of jeans but no item totaling more than $40. Just things I really needed.

I was shocked when I got my Visa bill. $600! No joke. I guess I did not realize how much I was spending with the rental car and all. Believe me, it's incredibly easy to run up a Visa bill without even knowing it.

My first lesson in banking: Keep good records, not only in your checkbook but also on your credit card. Lesson number two: Don't buy more than you can afford."

—Lauren Pass, Grossmont Community College

Budgeting goes hand-in-hand with banking. You and your parents should *write out* a spending plan. Be realistic and remember to include entertainment costs, housing, books, food, clothing, laundry, and lab fees.

Once at school, try to record daily expenditures in a budget book—for the first few weeks, anyway. When you realize how much you are spending on midnight pizzas and the local fast-food restaurant, you may think twice. A listing, in black-and-white, of how the money is evaporating, will force you to be fiscally aware and also prevent future catastrophes.

CHAPTER 24

Community Colleges

" *I was able to take community college classes during my senior year in high school. My experience was very positive. I took college-level classes and one college-prep class in English. I decided to enroll after high school. I wasn't sure what I wanted to major in and besides, my grandmother was paying my tuition. I am taking all college transfer classes now and have my plans made to transfer after two years. I also got a great part-time job through an internship, and since my college is near downtown, I can work after classes. I've met so many different people in my classes. I realize that I am young and have lots of learning to do. I am glad the community college was here for me."*

—Rachel Titus, Seattle Central Community College

" *Before my divorce was final, I knew I wanted to get back to the degree I had never finished. I found a community college in my area that had a strong college transfer program. There I was, the age of most of my fellow students' mothers, yet we all got along, worked to form study groups, and learned from each other. I graduated with honors on the dean's list, went on to get my B.A., and am now enrolled in a master's program to be a counselor."*

—Corrie Golub, Shoreline Community College

Why Go to Community College?

If you're starting your foray into higher education at a community college, you're in good company. Fifty percent of undergraduates in this country are in community colleges, just like you.

When you tell mom and dad or aunts and uncles that you are going to a community college they often are not sure what you mean. If they have not been watching the college scene in the past twenty years, they may be thinking about some junior college they heard of a long time ago that seemed to be for kids who had problems.

That's not you at all. You are a participant in one of the greatest experiments and adventures in higher education in this century. You are a part of a student body that spans all ages, races, languages, and levels of ability. You are enrolled in higher education that offers a tremendous amount of opportunity with smaller class sizes and a smaller price tag.

"Community" colleges do just that: they serve their communities. This means that you are probably living near home and attending a community college that is mostly a commuter school and does not house students in dorms, fraternities, or sororities.

These are the strengths of your community college:

1. You can live at home or on your own.
2. You can attend full-time or part-time, depending upon your situation. A large percentage of community college students work full- or part-time.
3. Your college is probably small enough that you can get involved in any kind of student activities that you wish.

How to Make the Best of Your Time

If you haven't already taken a look at the breadth of offerings at your college, this might be a good time to do it. Most community colleges have at least three kinds of programs that you can choose from:

1. COLLEGE PREPARATORY OR PRECOLLEGE PROGRAMS

Not all of the students who enter community college are writing, reading, or doing math at a college level. So, most community colleges test incoming students in these areas. If you need a brushup or review, you can get it at your community college.

Advice: If you need college-prep reading, English composition, or math, take those precollege classes early on—don't let them hold up your plans. For example, many students wait until they're ready to transfer before taking precollege math. The math class ends up being an unnecessary roadblock to transferring. By taking the college-prep courses early on, you also enable yourself to succeed in other classes. For instance, college-prep composition will help you to write better research papers and make you feel more comfortable during the writing sections of exams.

66 *I started community college several times. But the time I was successful, I started it by taking the math and English that I needed to get up to college-level. I moved quickly through the college-prep program and began to take college level courses. I finished my courses, transferred to the state university, and found that all of the good teaching I got had really helped me. I got my degree in business administration using the skills I had picked up studying with groups and being in small classes with instructor attention."*

—Jabari Grant, University of Washington

2. VOCATIONAL PROGRAMS

Most community colleges offer two-year vocational programs that lead directly into the job market. Many colleges are known for certain types of these programs. For example, some community colleges specialize in the biomedical field, computer technology, culinary arts, drafting, automotive, and so on. Check out the vocational programs at your community college. See if one of the fields interests you, especially if you are undecided about what kind of education you want and what you will do with it.

3. COLLEGE TRANSFER PROGRAMS

A large number of students are enrolled in community colleges to get the first two years of their college career in a smaller, less stressful environment that is more economical. If you fall into this category, here are some quick tips:

- See a college transfer counselor early on.
- Plan out your classes for your freshman and sophomore years to ensure you meet all the requirements.

- Make sure you are enrolling in transferable classes.
- Check out the transfer agreements between your college and universities in the area.
- Speak with representatives from four-year colleges when they visit your campus.
- If four-year college representatives do not visit, get in touch with the university where you want to transfer and find out about any unusual requirements.

Community colleges offer several degrees. Even if you are planning to transfer to a four-year college for your Bachelor of Arts (B.A.) degree, you still may want to consider an Associate of Arts (A.A.) degree. This A.A. degree is awarded when you accomplish what would be your freshman and sophomore years. It is great for putting on a resume or job application. Check out the requirements for an A.A. on your campus, and then decide if you want to try to meet those requirements. Some students just want to transfer to start working toward their B.A. and skip the A.A.

66 *I first started community college out of high school because it was the most economical choice for me. I did well in college transfer classes but did not have enough money to support myself. I left college and enrolled in a beauty school program. When I graduated, I got a job as a manicurist and returned to community college using my skills to support myself. I graduated with my A.A. and went on to major in economics and get my B.A. I supported myself the whole time. I even met my husband at the community college, and we transferred together. I now own my own business."*

—Jannette Hofmann, Seattle University

What Should You Take Advantage of While You Are at Community College?

1. SAVE MONEY FOR A RAINY DAY.

You are spending far less on a comparable education. Be aware of it! Save now, so you will have a cushion when you need it, perhaps while pursuing a more expensive education.

2. TAKE ADVANTAGE OF SMALLER CLASSES AND SMALLER STUDENT-TEACHER RATIOS.

Community colleges are known as teaching, not research, institutions. The instructors are hired to teach, not bury themselves in the library. You will have small classes in the 25 to 35 student range. These classes are taught by instructors who want to teach you—get to know them. Take classes from the instructors you like and avoid the ones you don't.

3. MEET OTHER STUDENTS.

Community colleges have diverse student bodies. Make an effort to meet the students in your classes. Form study groups. Don't be afraid of the woman who is your mother's age. (She may be the one getting the A's!) Learn about other cultures. Listen to the experiences of people who have been out there longer than you have.

4. GET INVOLVED IN ACTIVITIES.

A community college is small enough for you to get involved in student leadership or other activities. In the process, you will get to know other students and have a few items to fill in those blank spots on your resume or job applications.

66 *With two young children, I never thought I would be able to return to college. I went to a vocational training program, but I was disappointed in the training. A friend told me about Seattle Central*

Community College. I applied for financial aid and was accepted. I started school with no idea how I would do it, but by using all the resources available to me, I really did well. I took a few college-prep classes to review and I found that when I got into my college-level classes, I was the student getting A's and B's. I joined the National Honor Society with a chapter on my campus and, before I knew it, I was president. So here was me—single mother, honor society president, and, when I graduated with my A.A., I was chosen graduation speaker and given a scholarship. I don't know where I would have been without this opportunity."

—Georgette Brooks, University of Washington

CHAPTER 25

Working at School

" *A guy who lived in my dorm desperately wanted to find a job. But minimum wage, for him, was untenable. More simply, he wanted a job that would pay him adequately for his services.*

After several weeks of frantic job searching, nothing surfaced. Then, strolling merrily into my room one afternoon, he told me he'd found his pot of gold, a job that 'suited' him perfectly.

He had found employment in the arts—specifically, in the field of nude photography. And, let me just say, he wasn't the one taking the pictures.

While the job paid well, some of my more modest friends were paid equally well working graveyard shifts for a delivery service. Sure enough, if you're willing to endure unusual working conditions, healthy salaries are available."

—Steve Ojemann, University of Washington

Questions to Ask Before the Job Search

Before beginning a search for employment at college, ask yourself these five key questions:

1. WHY SHOULD YOU GET A JOB?

For some, the answer boils down to economics or, more specifically, the financing of a college education. For others, reasons for getting a job include work experience, references, and, of course, resume padding. Regardless of the specific reason, knowledge of why you are getting a job may help you answer the next question.

2. WHAT TYPE OF JOB SHOULD YOU GET?

Basically, three types of jobs exist: volunteer, research (which often yields college credit), and paid work.

The first category, volunteer work, bequeaths no money. But it often serves purposes more admirable than other types of employment. Having a volunteer job can lead to excellent future paying jobs, garner character recommendations, and look impressive on a resume.

The second type, in which college credit supersedes payment, takes some time to find but offers flexibility and, for the most part, no homework. A college advisor or job-placement service will ease the burden of a search for this type of job, often referred to as an assistantship, clerkship, or research preceptorship.

The final category of work includes all the miscellaneous jobs in which one is compensated for his or her services. Lack of experience may limit the job choices in this category to working in a fast-food restaurant or an equivalent. But don't fret! As you get older and more experienced, your opportunities will expand. In addition, you get to put a little extra money in your pocket, which is always a good thing.

A subdivision under the "paying job" category called "work-study" provides students demonstrating financial need with jobs paying higher-than-normal wages. These jobs, which require those interested to prove financial need, serve as pseudo-scholarships enabling some students to afford college. Generally, work-study jobs have the student working in a campus cafeteria or the office of a faculty member.

3. HOW MUCH TIME WILL THE JOB TAKE?

66 *Don't fool yourself. Any serious working schedule is going to take a huge chunk of time out of your day and force you to make some big sacrifices.*

But it can be done. I worked three jobs during college—at a pizza parlor, a men's clothing store, and in an athletic supply. In my free time, I even set up my own business. I had T-shirts made up and hired a crew to sell them for a profit. I paid for school that way.

I certainly wouldn't recommend this type of working schedule for everyone, though, especially if it starts negatively impacting your grades. See how much time you can afford to work and then go from there.

For me, it was a matter of making every second of every day count. I learned to manage my time so effectively that I could work over 30 hours a week, maintain decent grades, and even play varsity rugby. It mostly depends on the types of jobs you have and the type of person you are."

—Sean M. McTaggart, University of Pittsburgh

Before committing to any set number of hours, settle into a college schedule and determine the amount of study and free time available. Most employers sympathize with students and agree to a flexible work schedule with time off for midterms and finals.

The amount of time you have for work should depend on the number and difficulty of classes. Assuming a fairly standard college load of three or four classes, most working students agree that 10 to 20 hours a week is more than an ample time commitment for work.

A potential danger in working at school is getting involved in a job that requires time off the job or, more explicitly, job-related homework. Be wary of jobs that claim to demand only a fixed amount of time each week and then expect extra at-home work. Realize that certain jobs have unusual demands. University of Washington student John Schreuder warns, "A harmless flower-delivery job, which usually takes 3 hours a day, can become a nightmare on Mother's Day when deliveries increase tenfold."

4. SHOULD YOU GET AN ON-CAMPUS OR OFF-CAMPUS JOB?

There are three major factors you need to take into account before answering this question: desirability, wages, and transportation. Basically, you want to obtain the most desirable job that is easy to get to with the highest wages.

At large universities, on-campus jobs of this sort may be plentiful. At smaller private schools, however, finding a desirable on-campus job may be more difficult. But, before going off campus, make sure to consider transportation. You don't want to be walking 8 miles to work at 5 A.M. because no other means of transportation are available.

5. WHAT ARE SOME JOBS YOU CAN GET?

Now that you have some questions to hash over, you undoubtedly are interested in what specific jobs are available to college students. While off-campus jobs vary depending upon the setting of the campus, on-campus jobs remain fairly similar throughout the country.

Attractive benefits of these university-sponsored jobs include reasonable pay and flexible hours. Several common university-sponsored jobs include:

Food service jobs: Duties include serving meals, preparing food, and performing custodial work.

University libraries: Libraries always need people to help with checking out and reshelving books.

Tutoring positions: Many larger schools have a student tutoring service sponsored by the university.

Recreational sports programs: This usually involves managing and organizing intramural sports activities.

Ticket offices: Most colleges have at least one or two ticket outlets for sporting and special events such as plays and art exhibitions.

Copy centers: Universities often use students to staff copy centers because barely any experience is needed to fulfill the post.

Parking division: This includes enforcing parking rules on campus and running visitor parking facilities.

Residence halls: Employment in a residence hall may range from clerical to custodial work. Resident advisers (RAs) also are needed.

Clerical work: Many departments need students who have office skills such as typing.

Ground maintenance: In this line of work, duties may vary from gardening to custodial or even window washing.

Psst . . . If you are lucky, you can find work doing something you ordinarily would do for free. For example, many college newspapers and yearbooks offer salaried positions for writers and editors. Many would-be journalists can make a pretty penny doing something they love.

In addition, the advertising departments of campus publications are always looking for advertising representatives. These jobs usually pay well, offering you a percentage of your sales.

Trying the Entrepreneurial Route

❝ *Our tennis team needed money for equipment, so I decided to put my entrepreneurial talents to the test. I obtained the rights from both the Lowenbrau beer corporation and UPS to use their logos. Then I bought 200 mugs and put the Lowenbrau and UPS insignias on all 200. The team sold the mugs at the fall season football games, and I made a nice profit for the team."*

—Keith Vernon, University of Puget Sound

If the typical jobs don't appeal to you, you can try the entrepreneurial route. College students have made more than pocket change selling T-shirts, mugs, Greek swimsuit calendars, videos of the campus, and so on.

An entrepreneur always thinks in terms of supply and demand, a true capitalist to the end. If something is needed at your school, the successful entrepreneur provides it—at a price, of course!

Keep in mind that entrepreneurial schemes are risky. If you really need the money for tuition or books, some of the other jobs are more practical.

Where Do You Look and Who Do You Ask?

In many cases, the answer to where to look for a job should be apparent. For example, if a volunteer job in the health sciences is the goal, simply contact a local hospital. On the other hand, if no specific job has distinguished itself, several resources might help. Following is a list of three resources at your disposal.

1. FRIENDS AND RELATIVES

The best source of job information comes from word-of-mouth communication; someone tells you about a job opening, and you pursue it.

Friends and family members can be invaluable when it comes to this kind of information. Once they know you are searching for a job, they may notice ads in the newspaper or signs in windows. More often, a friend or relative may know someone who has a job opening and may be able to "pull a few strings" for you. You have heard the expression: It doesn't matter what you know but who you know. Well, the expression didn't get famous for nothing!

2. UNIVERSITY RESOURCES

Most universities have a career placement office through which you can find some invaluable information. Counselors in these offices can help you locate a job and give you some advice on applying for one as well.

In addition, many schools have computer systems that contain listings of job openings classified and referenced by job type, location, pay, applicant's experience, and various other criteria. At many large schools, the computer list of jobs is updated daily and contains valuable information such as the employer's telephone number and time commitment desired. You probably don't even have to leave your room to access this job database. Most schools make this database available to students via their Web site.

3. OTHER PLACES TO LOOK

In most cases, employers will post signs, take out ads in a newspaper, or in some way make "public" their desire for employees. If you have your heart set on working for a specific company that is not advertising, calling and asking for a job never hurts; the employer might be impressed that you took the initiative.

Applying for the Job

For most university-sponsored jobs such as food service, you will not need to apply. You may just call up an office and be told to meet at the job site in the morning.

But for more prestigious university jobs and summer employment, the application process is crucial.

Still, the most helpful piece of advice available is, "Don't worry!" Everyone has faced rejection—more than once—and lived to tell about it. Don't let your lack of experience invoke anguish. As University of Washington sophomore Katie MacDonald said, "If they are offering a job to students, usually they don't expect a rocket scientist. If they get someone who is honest and reliable, they're happy."

The following sections provide tips on job applications, interviews, and resumes. Pay special attention to the sample resume and cover letter as both will come in handy if you are writing your own.

1. JOB APPLICATION

Although varied in specific form, job applications contain several customary questions. Most applications ask for certain character references, which usually means former employers. In the case of a first job, naming teachers or high school counselors is acceptable.

Most employers will contact a reference if one is provided, so notify the person that he or she may receive a phone call from the prospective employer.

2. THE JOB INTERVIEW

Contrary to the premonitions of most students, job interviews are not the most stressful part of the process. When an employer asks to interview a potential employee, it generally means that the applicant has a chance of being hired.

Remember to project your best side at these meetings. There is no use in accentuating the negative sides of your character, unless the employer asks.

Psst . . . Although it is better to overdress than underdress when interviewing, a sports jacket and slacks will suffice in almost any setting, except if you are interviewing for a job on Wall Street or the like. Obviously, when applying for a house-painting job, lifeguarding, construction, or McDonald's, your attire could be even less formal.

3. WRITING A RESUME

A polished resume becomes crucial in the adult world. Even in college, top-notch employers demand one.

Most word processing programs come with several different resume templates. It takes about 20 minutes to create your own resume using one of these templates—check it out!

Employers usually prefer short and to-the-point resumes. One page with all pertinent personal information should suffice; if your resume exceeds one page, cut out the least important material. A cover letter also should be included.

(See the sample resume and cover letter on pages 236 and 237.)

How Do You Apply for Work-Study Jobs?

Not everyone can get a work-study job, but anyone can apply.

The first step in applying, as with all other forms of financial aid, is to submit a standardized Free Application for Federal Student Aid (FAFSA), obtainable from high school and college counseling offices. The College Scholarship Board then will inform applicants of the status of their application.

Once accepted into the work-study program, the student can choose from available positions and determine the times he or she wants to work. Because work-study usually serves as a form of financial aid, compensation for work may go directly to the university to cover tuition and housing. This depends on the specific program and the need of the student as determined by the board.

Wait a Second! Do You Even Want a Job?

66 *I chose not to work my first year at school, and I'm glad I didn't. For me, there were just too many things I wanted to do when I first arrived. Having a job would have taken a huge chunk of time out of a day with too few hours in it already.*

During your freshman year, there are going to be so many new people you are going to want to meet. There are going to be hundreds of activities around campus that you should try out. Besides that, you have to account for studying—oh, and sleeping too. For me, I had to make time for the soccer team as well.

I don't know what I will do sophomore year. But, if you can help it, not working during your freshman year is definitely something to think about."

—Heidi Wiedemann, Duke University

Many students feel working at school is too big a sacrifice. Before committing to any job, no matter how wonderful it may be, remember that school should come first . . . that's usually what you are trying to pay for anyway.

Despite this cautionary note, realize that many successful students have found it perfectly possible and even enjoyable to work and study simultaneously.

One More Thing! About That Summer Job . . .

Some students choose not to work during the school year, but most college students find some kind of gainful employment during the summer.

For some students, summer employment is no big source of stress. If you know that you will be going home for the summer to work for a former employer or if you will be going back to camp to be a counselor again, then you can relax.

But if you are planning to move on to something new next summer, you will want to plan ahead, especially if you are planning to work in a different city, in which case you will need to make arrangements for living accommodations as well.

Try to have a general idea of your summer plans by winter break. The earlier you decide, the more opportunities will be available. Many summer internship programs have applications that are due during the winter, and you will want to have plenty of time to fill out the necessary forms.

Your school's career center or employment counseling office should have information on summer opportunities, so stop by and see what you can find. Failing that, look at the library for internship guides. Older students are also a great resource. If you hear a student talking about this awesome job he or she had last summer, then you might ask for the name of someone to talk to at that particular company.

You have three summers during college, so don't be afraid to get creative. If you've always wanted to work in Washington, D.C., don't hesitate to contact your U.S. representative or senator. If you want to live it up in the Big Apple, find out about opportunities for internships there. If a Hollywood film set is more your style, write to some production companies or surf the Web for opportunities in LA.

Whatever you do, plan ahead. Otherwise, come May, the relief of finishing finals may be tainted by the uncertainty of your summer employment.

SAMPLE COVER LETTER

November 23, 2002

Barney Rubbish
Bedrock University
Bedrock, Maine 04035
456-867-5309

Mr. Wayne Bruce
BAT CAVE ACCESSORIES
10001 Batcave Avenue, Suite 13
Gotham City, North Dakota 01928

Dear Mr. Bruce:

I am interested in the internship your company offers college undergraduates who are pursuing a career in cave carving.

Presently, I am a freshman at Bedrock University, where I plan to major in geology. As you can see from the enclosed resume, I have had experience working as a rock cutter for Fred Flinstein Rock Cutting on a part-time basis. I am considering cave carving as a long-range career possibility.

Please send me all relevant information with regard to the internship. If you have any questions, do not hesitate to call me at 456-867-5309.

Thank you for your time, and I look forward to speaking with you soon.

Sincerely,

Barney Rubbish

SAMPLE RESUME

BARNEY RUBBISH

Present Address:
Bedrock University
Bedrock, Maine 04035
456-555-5309
barney@bedrock.edu

Permanent Address:
1111 11th Avenue, SE
Big Apple, New York 20212
212-555-7890

Objective: To obtain a position as a rock cutter with a corporate firm.

Education:

9/97–present   Bedrock University, Bedrock, Maine. Course work includes: geology, rock cutting, earth science, and dinosaur training. Major: geology. GPA: 4.0

8/93–6/97   Big Apple High School, Big Apple, New York. GPA: 4.0

Work Experience:

6/97–present   **Dinosaur Trainer,** Bedrock Museum, Bedrock, Maine. Trained dinosaurs to do dog tricks at Bedrock Museum.

6/95–9/96   **Assistant Rock Cutter,** Fred Flinstein Rock Cutting, Bedrock, Maine.

Honors/Awards: Wilma Flinstein Science Award
Dean's List, Bedrock University
Member of Dinosaur Bone Collecting Club

Skills: Word processing, computer graphics

Foreign Languages: Spanish, Sanskrit

References: Jack N. DeBeanstock
Giant Beanstocks, Inc.
133 121st Avenue
Metropolis, New York 20213
212-867-2233
jack@rcomail.com

CHAPTER 26

Commuting

66 *I graduated early from high school—right after junior year. At 17, the thought of living away from home seemed overwhelming and scary. Besides, I wasn't really into the big "party scene" that seemed to go along with campus life."*

—Kira Lehner, Hofstra University

66 *My university doesn't have any dorms, so there wasn't a whole lot of choice about commuting. However, I did know that I wanted to live away from home, so I opted for off-campus housing. St. John's has advertisements for nearby apartments posted in Marillac Hall, so I just kept checking until I found one that was right for me. To me, it was the best of both worlds: being able to commute to school and still having the independence of being out on my own."*

—Susan Bolster, St. John's University

Not everybody lives at school. In fact, if you are not considering commuting your freshman year, you probably will at some point during your college career.

There are several advantages to commuting. Some students can find cheaper housing away from campus. Others prefer living outside the campus environment, whether it be with a few friends in an apartment in a nearby city, or with their parents in the comforts of home. Some need to work and have a job that is not located near their college. Regardless of your reasons for commuting, here are some tips to keep in mind.

Set Your Alarm Clock

If you're a commuter, set your alarm clock and leave early. Students who live on campus don't have to deal with bus schedules, traffic, or finding a parking spot. You do! And sometimes that's not such an easy task.

❝ *Probably the worst thing about commuting to USC was the traffic. I never knew how bad it was going to be. Sometimes it took me an hour to get to school, other times only 15 minutes. I ended up always leaving an hour early and bringing extra work in case I had some time before class."*

—Shannon Strasser, University of Southern California

 Psst . . . At most colleges, students who commute by car have to apply and pay for parking privileges. Find out about parking before you start school. Finding vacant spots on campus or on side streets is often difficult and can be dangerous, especially in questionable neighborhoods.

Pick the Right Schedule

This is especially important for commuters. Avoid scheduling your first class at 9:00 A.M. and your second at 1:30 P.M. Although some commuters may be able to go home in the lapse, many will not. Passing four or five hours on campus can be rough when you don't have a dorm room or anywhere to unwind.

❝ *For several semesters I managed to get all my classes on Tuesdays and Thursdays (taking an evening class if necessary). Besides the luxury of going to school two days a week. I had the time to get a much-needed part-time job."*

—Eric Hafker, Queens College

Try To Stay in Touch With Campus Life

66 *As a commuter, I was nervous that I would never meet any other students or have any connection with USC. So, I made a concerted effort to try to meet people in my classes. To my surprise, it was pretty easy. I met two other commuters on the first day. Both of them were feeling the same way I did. Now we meet for lunch on campus about two times a week. I feel a lot more comfortable walking around campus knowing that I have a few good friends."*

—Shannon Strasser, University of Southern California

It's common to feel lost or out-of-touch your freshman year, especially if you attend a large college. For commuters, who lack the opportunity of socializing in the dorms or Greek houses, assimilating can be an even tougher challenge. Here are a few tips to help you cure the commuter blues.

1. DON'T GO HOME AS SOON AS CLASSES ARE OVER.

If you have free time after class, take a walk around campus and visit the student center. Most student centers will have a bulletin board with job listings, summer internships, and local sports and social opportunities. Your college may also have a commuter club that sponsors social events specifically for commuters.

2. SET UP A CARPOOL.

Carpooling is an excellent way to meet other commuters. Most schools will have listings of other students living in your area who want to carpool—check with your school's parking administration office, commuter club, or student center. As an added bonus, many schools will actually reduce your parking fee if you join a carpool.

3. SET UP DATES WITH PEOPLE YOU MEET ON CAMPUS.

One way to force yourself to get involved in the campus community is to set up dates with other students you meet in class or on campus. Plan to meet someone for lunch in your school's cafeteria or deli. Study over a cup of coffee at a local cafe. Remember that you are not alone. Most students—commuters especially—will welcome the chance to get to know a new person on campus.

4. TAKE ADVANTAGE OF YOUR SCHOOL'S OFFERINGS.

College will afford you hundreds of opportunities that you may never have again. Before you leave, make sure you attend at least one campus play, art show, music performance, or sports event. Use the library and computer resources. Attend a lecture in a subject that sounds interesting. Just because you're a commuter doesn't mean that you have to miss out completely on your "college experience."

66 *The toughest thing for me about being a commuter was breaking out of my shell. I remember spending a lot of my free time freshman year studying in the library or just going home early. It was tough to hang around school when you didn't know anyone.*

Gradually I began to realize that little things could make a big difference, like eating in the cafeteria when I was by myself, hanging out in the student center, and studying outside on the benches instead of cooped up in the library. Running into classmates and getting familiar with the campus helped me to open up, make more friends, and get more involved in activities."

—Christina Buffamonte, Hofstra University

Epilogue

College provides a cushioned entrance to the real world. While you don't have to pay taxes or hold down a full-time job, you still will be learning basic survival skills, the ones detailed in previous chapters. Indeed, college is your first step toward real independence.

The road to graduation is not always straight; there will be peaks, valleys, and curves. But if you set some goals, keep your chin up, maintain a sense of humor, and have fun in the process, college truly can be "four of the best years of your life."

 Psst . . . In the tritest of terms, we hope you had as much fun reading this book as we did writing it. And if you learned something in the process, that's even better. We know we did.

Greg Gottesman, Daniel Baer, and the rest of the gang

COLLEGE SURVIVAL TEAR-OUT CHECKLIST

This is an extensive checklist of essentials you will need to survive at college. Some items may not apply to you, but make sure to include those that do! Remember that for some items it might be easier to pick them up once you get to school!

Clothing

UNDERWEAR, SOCKS, PAJAMAS, ETC.

- ❏ Bath robe
- ❏ Pajamas
- ❏ Socks (plenty)
- ❏ Undershirts
- ❏ Underwear (plenty)
- ❏ Bras
- ❏ Slips
- ❏ Tights

CASUAL WEAR

- ❏ Bathing suit
- ❏ Belts
- ❏ Blue jeans (perfect for any climate)
- ❏ Heavy coat
- ❏ Lightweight jacket
- ❏ Long-sleeved shirts
- ❏ Shorts (depends on climate)
- ❏ Slacks (such as khaki pants)
- ❏ Tank tops
- ❏ T-shirts (you can never have too many)
- ❏ Sweaters
- ❏ Sweatshirts (get one from the alma mater)

❏ Sweatsuits

❏ Turtle necks

❏ Dresses

❏ Purses

❏ Skirts

❏ Blouses

❏ Baseball cap/hat

OUTERWEAR FOR COLDER CLIMATES

❏ Earmuffs

❏ Gloves or mittens

❏ Parka

❏ Raincoat

❏ Scarf

❏ Umbrella

FORMAL WEAR

❏ Dress socks

❏ Sports jacket and slacks

❏ Tie

❏ Evening bag

❏ Evening dress

❏ Panty hose

SHOES

❏ Athletic shoes

❏ Casual shoes

❏ Dress shoes

❏ Flats

❏ Heels

❏ Flip-flops (shower shoes)

JEWELRY

❐ Earrings

❐ Necklaces

❐ Pins

❐ Rings

❐ Watches

BATHROOM BUDDIES: TOWELS AND COSMETICS

❐ Baby powder

❐ Cologne or perfume

❐ Contacts, solution, and case

❐ Conditioner

❐ Cotton balls

❐ Dental floss

❐ Deodorant

❐ Hairbrushes

❐ Hair spray

❐ Kleenex

❐ Mousse

❐ Nail clippers

❐ Nail file

❐ Q-tips

❐ Razors

❐ Retainers and mouthguards

❐ Shampoo

❐ Shaving cream

❐ Soap (face and body)

❐ Suntan or skin lotion

❐ Toothbrush

❐ Toothpaste

❐ Towels

❏ Tweezers

❏ Washcloths

❏ Barrettes, hair bows, rubber bands, etc.

❏ Makeup

❏ Makeup remover

❏ Nail polish

❏ Nail polish remover

❏ Feminine hygiene products

MEDICAL SUPPLIES

❏ Ace bandage

❏ Alka Seltzer

❏ Aspirin or pain relievers

❏ Band-Aids

❏ Contraceptives

❏ Cough drops

❏ Decongestant

❏ Emergency kit

❏ Hydrogen Peroxide

❏ Laxative

❏ Rubbing alcohol

❏ Sun screen

❏ Thermometer

SPORTS GEAR

❏ Baseball glove

❏ Baseball, football, soccer ball (optional)

❏ Frisbee

❏ Skis and appropriate wardrobe

❏ Rackets

Room Essentials

BED BASICS

- ❏ Bedspread or comforter
- ❏ Blankets
- ❏ Pillow
- ❏ Sheets and pillowcases
- ❏ Sleeping bag (optional)
- ❏ Mattress pad

YOUR ACADEMIC HEADQUARTERS: SCHOOL SUPPLIES

- ❏ Alarm clock
- ❏ Backpack
- ❏ Calculator (preferably solar)
- ❏ Calendar (with lots of writing space)
- ❏ Envelopes
- ❏ Highlighters
- ❏ Notebook paper
- ❏ Paper clips
- ❏ Pencils
- ❏ Pencil sharpener
- ❏ Pens
- ❏ Ruler
- ❏ Scissors
- ❏ Stamps
- ❏ Stapler and staples
- ❏ Stationery
- ❏ Tape

BOOKS

☐ A respected dictionary
Suggestion: *American Heritage or Webster's*

☐ A foreign language dictionary, if you plan to study a language

☐ A thesaurus or synonym-finder, preferably in easy dictionary form
Suggestion: *Roget's International Thesaurus*

☐ A bible, not necessarily for religious purposes

☐ A book on the rules of English grammar
Suggestion: *The Elements of Style* by William Strunk, Jr. and E.B. White
  or, *The Chicago Manual of Style* by The University of Chicago Press

☐ A book of quotations
Suggestion: *Bartlett's Book of Quotations*

LIGHTING

☐ Desk light
☐ Bed light

COMPUTERS

☐ Computer and printer (optional but recommended)

Making Extra Space: Storage, Closets and Organization

The following items are optional:

☐ Baskets
☐ Bookshelves
☐ Hangers
☐ Hooks—large and small
☐ Loft material
☐ Trunk

❏ Under-the-bed storage boxes

❏ Waste can

Curing the Munchies

The following items are optional:

❏ Blender

❏ Glasses, mugs, and plastic cups

❏ Hot pot

❏ Microwave

❏ Popcorn popper

❏ Small refrigerator

❏ Toaster oven

❏ Utensils (bottle opener, spoons, forks, knives, and napkins)

Miscellaneous

The following items are optional:

❏ Answering machine

❏ Drying rack for clothing

❏ Extension cord

❏ Fan (necessary for warm climates)

❏ Iron and board

❏ Laundry basket

❏ Surge protector

❏ Telephone

❏ Tool kit (for example: hammer, nails, screwdrivers, screws, thumbtacks, picture hooks, tape measure, duct tape)

Additional Items You Want to Take

AUTHORS

GREG GOTTESMAN
School: Stanford University

Major: Political Science

Hobbies: Tennis, journalism, government, writing college books

Piece of Advice: "Be yourself, unless no one else can stand you."

DANIEL BAER
School: Harvard University

Major: Social Studies/Afro American Studies

Hobbies: Skiing, writing, jogging

Piece of Advice: "Study hard, but don't forget to ditch the books and relax in the sun every once in a while. Finish your papers, but don't forget to leave the computer and talk into the night with a close friend every once in a while. Lose yourself in the excitement, but don't forget to take a step back and gain perspective every once in a while."

CARTOONIST

STEVE OJEMANN
School: University of Washington

Major: Political Science/Biology

Hobbies: Water-skiing, drawing, philosophy

Piece of Advice: "A very popular error: having the courage of one's convictions; rather it is a matter of having the courage for an attack on one's convictions."—Friedrich Nietzsche

CONTRIBUTORS

RICO ALEXANDER
School: Stanford University
Major: Biology/Pre-med
Hobbies: Volleyball, tennis, basketball, Nintendo
Piece of Advice: "Free your mind, and your ass will follow."—George Clinton

RICK ARNEY
School: Stanford University
Major: Economics/Political Science
Hobbies: Going to A's games, driving, writing, badminton
Piece of Advice: "Don't forget your parents."

CHRISTINA BUFFAMONTE
School: Hofstra University
Major: Publishing Studies & Literature
Hobbies: Drawing, reading, writing, music
Piece of Advice: "Have fun experimenting with a wide variety of courses—not just the ones related to your major."

PADDY CARSON
School: University of Colorado at Boulder
Major: Broadcast production management
Hobbies: Skiing, life
Piece of Advice: "There's so much more to college than academics, but in order to experience more, you have to stay in school."

BRYAN COHEN
School: Claremont McKenna College
Major: History/Government
Hobbies: Music, nudity, fish, drama, government
Piece of Advice: "Don't take life so seriously, or you will implode."

MATT CRILE

School: University of Washington

Major: International business

Hobbies: Rugby, reading, guitar

Piece of Advice: "Don't ever change to suit someone else."

LESLIE FRIEND

School: University of Chicago

Major: Music

Hobbies: Playing the cello, tennis

Piece of Advice: "Work as hard as you play, and play as hard as you work."

ANDY GOTTESMAN

School: University of Michigan

Major: Political Science/Communication

Hobbies: Writing, reading, baseball

Piece of Advice: "College is sharing Oreos and hot chocolate with friends after a Michigan victory on a crisp, sunny football Saturday."

JESSICA HALL

School: Syracuse University

Major: Magazine Journalism

Hobbies: Writing, photography

Piece of Advice: "Resist the urge to count down the days until winter or spring break. Ninety-seven days and counting will only depress you."

TARA MCCANN

School: Stanford University

Major: Political Science/Communication

Hobbies: Piano, dance, movies, parasailing

Piece of Advice: "The majority of my college education didn't come from text books and lectures but from 3 A.M. discussions with friends and heated debates with the guy down the hall."

THOM MCDADE

School: Pomona College

Major: Biosocial Anthropology

Hobbies: Skiing, backpacking, river rafting

Piece of Advice: "Get involved at your school whether it be athletics, academic clubs, or social awareness groups. Play an active role in the community. It's a great way to make friends."

WHITNEY B. MORRIS

School: Pomona College

Major: Government

Hobbies: Dance, skiing, rugby

Piece of Advice: "Studying isn't enough. Join organizations and groups that interest you. Become involved in your college community."

TAMI OSTROFF

School: Pomona College

Major: Anthropology

Hobbies: Dance, watching sports, hanging out

Piece of Advice: "Be open-minded and don't have specific expectations."

JAMIE REYNOLDS

School: Stanford University

Major: English/Latin American Studies

Hobbies: Basketball, theater (technical), singing, foreign beer connoisseur

Piece of Advice: "Relax and take it easy. Let college adapt to your pace. Remember you're the one who's paying."

STANLEY RYTER

School: University of Washington

Major: Civil Engineering

Hobbies: Skiing, basketball, hiking, traveling, government

Piece of Advice: "If at first you don't succeed, ask her out again."

JOHN GERARD SCHREUDER

School: University of Washington

Major: Bioengineering

Hobbies: Sports, photography, travel

Piece of Advice: "Don't waste your college years by taking school too seriously."

DAVID STERN

School: Cornell University

Major: Government/English

Hobbies: Cycling, tennis, reading

Piece of Advice: "Take a year off to do something other than go to school for four years—spend a year abroad, work, travel."

MARTINA STEWART

School: Yale University

Major: English/African-American Studies

Hobbies: Moviebuffery, figure skating, aerobics (step, slide, and funk)

Piece of Advice: "You've gotta live on the edge. Otherwise, you're just taking up space."

KEITH VERNON

School: University of Puget Sound

Major: Business/Finance

Hobbies: Money, tennis, skiing, people

Piece of Advice: "If you exert yourself 100 percent, you can never be disappointed with your results."

NOELEEN WALDER

School: Stanford University

Major: Psychology/Visual Anthropology

Hobbies: Photography, reading, writing, stressing out

Piece of Advice: "Don't stress out about a major. Try a lot of different areas before you settle down into one."

CONAN YUAN

School: Harvard University

Major: Computer Engineering

Hobbies: Music (playing, singing, listening), tennis

Piece of Advice: "All computer problems are simple—they're just clouded in jargon."

NOTES

NOTES